D1189604

The NFL National Anthem Protests

Recent Title in
21st-Century Turning Points

The #MeToo Movement
Laurie Collier Hillstrom

The NFL National Anthem Protests

Margaret Haerens

21st-Century Turning Points

 ABC-CLIO™

An Imprint of ABC-CLIO, LLC
Santa Barbara, California • Denver, Colorado

Copyright © 2019 by ABC-CLIO, LLC

Library of Congress Cataloging in Publication Control Number: 2018043938

ISBN: 978–1–4408–6903–7 (print)
     978–1–4408–6904–4 (ebook)

23 22 21 20 19   1 2 3 4 5

This book is also available as an eBook.

ABC-CLIO
An Imprint of ABC-CLIO, LLC

ABC-CLIO, LLC
130 Cremona Drive, P.O. Box 1911
Santa Barbara, California 93116-1911
www.abc-clio.com

This book is printed on acid-free paper ∞

Manufactured in the United States of America

Contents

Series Foreword   ix

Chapter 1   **Overview of the NFL National Anthem Protests**   1

Chapter 2   **Landmark Events**   11
  "The Star-Spangled Banner" Is Played at a Sporting
    Event for the First Time (1918)   11
  "The Star-Spangled Banner" Becomes the
    National Anthem (1931)   14
  The NFL Mandates the National Anthem Be Played
    before Games (1945)   17
  Smith and Carlos Give the Black Power Salute at the
    Olympic Games (1968)   20
  The Olympic Games Protest (1972)   23
  The NBA Suspends Mahmoud Abdul-Rauf for Not
    Standing during the Anthem (1996)   26
  The NFL Mandates Players Be on the Field for the
    National Anthem (2009)   29
  St. Louis Rams Protest Police Brutality (2014)   33
  University of Missouri Protests Force President's
    Resignation (2015)   36
  Colin Kaepernick Refuses to Stand for the
    National Anthem (2016)   41
  Trump Calls for the Firing of Protesting
    NFL Players (2017)   43
  NFL Protests Spread in Response to Trump
    Criticisms (2017)   46
  The NFL Creates a Controversial New Anthem
    Policy (2018)   50

The White House Cancels Its Super Bowl
    Championship Celebration (2018)   54

Chapter 3   **Impacts of the NFL National Anthem Protests**   59
                 NFL Protests Impact Corporate Sponsors   59
                 NFL Protests Affect National Politics   64
                 Impact on Other Sports Leagues   68
                 Debates on Patriotism and Constitutional Rights   73
                 How People Perceive the National Anthem   76
                 NFL Protests and Race Relations   80
                 Issues of Racial Inequality and Police Brutality   84
                 The NFL's Image and Popularity   88

Chapter 4   **Profiles**   95
                 Boyer, Nate (1981–)   95
                     Former NFL player and military veteran
                     who inspired Colin Kaepernick to kneel in protest
                 Goodell, Roger (1959–)   98
                     NFL Commissioner since 2006
                 Jenkins, Malcolm (1987–)   101
                     NFL player who knelt in protest in 2016 and
                     cofounded the Players Coalition
                 Johnson, Christopher (1959–)   104
                     Chairman and CEO of the New York Jets who
                     chose not to fine or suspend protesting players
                 Jones, Jerry (1942–)   107
                     Owner, president, and general manager of the Dallas
                     Cowboys who claimed NFL protests negatively
                     affect the league
                 Kaepernick, Colin (1987–)   110
                     Former NFL player and the first player to kneel
                     in protest during the National Anthem
                 Kraft, Robert (1941–)   115
                     New England Patriots owner who supported players'
                     right to protest but remained concerned about financial
                     implications for the league
                 Long, Chris (1985–)   117
                     First white NFL player to participate in protests
                     during the National Anthem

Reid, Eric (1991–)   121
  Former teammate of Colin Kaepernick and
  second NFL player to kneel in protest during the
  National Anthem
Trump, Donald J. (1946–)   124
  Forty-fifth U.S. president, who made the NFL protests a
  national political issue by criticizing protesting players
Villanueva, Alejandro (1988–)   127
  Pittsburgh Steelers player who stood visibly at the front
  of the players' tunnel during the National Anthem while
  teammates remained out of sight inside the tunnel

Further Resources   131

Index   135

Series Foreword

21st-Century Turning Points is a general reference series that has been crafted for use by high school and undergraduate students as well as members of the general public. The purpose of the series is to give readers a clear, authoritative, and unbiased understanding of major fast-breaking events, movements, people, and issues that are transforming American life, culture, and politics in this turbulent new century. Each volume constitutes a one-stop resource for learning about a single issue or event currently dominating America's news headlines and political discussions—issues or events that, in many cases, are also driving national debate about our country's leaders, institutions, values, and priorities.

Each volume in the *21st-Century Turning Points* series begins with an **Overview** of the event or issue that is the subject of the book. It then provides a suite of informative chronologically arranged narrative entries on specific **Landmarks** in the evolution of the event or issue in question. This section provides both vital historical context and insights into present-day news events to give readers a full and clear understanding of how current issues and controversies evolved.

The next section of the book is devoted to examining the **Impacts** of the event or issue in question on various aspects of American life, including political, economic, cultural, and interpersonal implications. It is followed by a chapter of biographical **Profiles** that summarize the life experiences and personal beliefs of prominent individuals associated with the event or issue in question.

Finally, each book concludes with a topically organized **Further Resources** list of important and informative resources—from influential books to fascinating websites—to which readers can turn for additional information, and a carefully compiled subject **Index**.

These complementary elements, found in every book in the series, work together to create an evenhanded, authoritative, and user-friendly tool for gaining a deeper and more accurate understanding of the fast-changing nation in which we live—and the issues and moments that define us as we move deeper into the twenty-first century.

CHAPTER ONE

Overview of the NFL National Anthem Protests

"I am not going to stand up to show pride in a flag for a country that oppresses black people and people of color" (Wyche 2016). With these words, Colin Kaepernick, a quarterback for the San Francisco 49ers, explained his decision to protest what he saw as the systematic oppression of people of color, especially several deadly incidents of police brutality against African American men. An image of his protest—sitting alone on a sidelines bench during the national anthem before his team's August 26, 2016, preseason game against the Green Bay Packers—was captured by Jennifer Lee Chan, a beat writer for *NinersNation.com*.

After the game, Chan tweeted the photo. It went viral, prompting international media attention and inspiring intense national debates over issues of racial inequality, police brutality, patriotism, and social justice activism's role in sports. Inflamed by presidential commentary, political partisanship, and racial biases, these conversations catapulted National Football League (NFL) officials, team owners, and players into the crosshairs of a consuming controversy. NFL football became the most polarizing professional sport in the United States.

The Role of Black Protest in Sports

Kaepernick's solo protests in early 2016 49ers games grew into a significant movement in the history of black activism and protest in sports. Since the racial integration of all professional American sports leagues in the twentieth century, black athletes gained an invaluable platform for making their voices heard on social justice and racism. The rise of black activism and protest in sport was part of a larger effort toward black empowerment, racial equality, and the elimination of institutional racial discrimination that profoundly changed American consciousness in the 1960s.

One of the first major black sports figures to garner international attention for his protests was legendary American boxer, Muhammad Ali (1942–2016). An Olympic gold medalist and heavyweight champion, Ali used his fame and renowned wit and charm to advocate for black pride and empowerment. In 1966, Ali, who had converted to Islam, refused to be drafted by the U.S. Army to fight in the Vietnam War, citing religious objections. He was arrested, found guilty of draft evasion, and stripped of his boxing titles. Eventually, in 1971, the U.S. Supreme Court upheld his right to be a conscientious objector, or someone who refuses to serve in the armed forces or bear arms. Ali's strong religious and moral objections to war as well as his lifelong support of civil rights and black pride inspired generations of black activists all over the world.

By the late 1960s, growing opposition to the Vietnam War as well as racial unrest resulted in race riots and political protests throughout the United States. Sports reflected the political and social turmoil of U.S. society. During the 1968 Summer Olympics in Mexico City, two African American track-and-field stars, Tommie Smith and John Carlos, raised their fists in a black power salute while receiving their medals. This action drew death threats and a suspension from the U.S. track team but also won praise and admiration from other black athletes. The image of Smith and Carlos with fists upraised is iconic in U.S. sports history. It inspired a similar protest during the 1972 Summer Olympics, when U.S. track-and-field stars Wayne Collett and Vince Matthews also protested during the ceremony when receiving their medals.

As black athletes gained prominence and attained success in professional sports, they continued to use their public platform to exercise their right to free speech on social, political, and racial issues. However, league officials and team owners showed mixed reactions to this activism. This can be seen in the National Basketball Association (NBA). On one hand, the NBA, a league with many African American players, supported activists, including Kareem Abdul-Jabbar and Bill Russell. On the other hand, in 1996 the NBA issued a suspension for Denver Nuggets player Mahmoud Abdul-Rauf after he refused to stand for the national anthem, citing moral and religious objections. Abdul-Rauf was able to forge a compromise with the league—he would stand for the anthem but be allowed to silently pray during it. In recent years, the NBA has been actively involved in supporting causes and movements important to African American players, and this support has been credited with fostering a positive relationship between all parties. Similarly, current players like LeBron James, Dwyane Wade, and Chris Paul have raised awareness of social injustice and racial issues while maintaining the support of team owners and top NBA officials.

Football and Activism

In the United States, football is arguably the most popular sport. Much of the National Football League's success has been attributed to its carefully constructed, conservative, all-American image, a brand that appeals to many. The league's long association with patriotism can be traced back to 1945, when NFL Commissioner Elmer Layden adopted the custom of playing "The Star-Spangled Banner" as a way to unite fans, players, and officials before every game. In 1978, the policy of playing the anthem during pregame activities was formally set down in the NFL's game operations manual, but players were allowed to remain in the locker room until the start of each game. As the NFL featured more and more military events—Air Force flyovers, veteran appreciation ceremonies, military-band performances—NFL players were required to participate.

In 2015, the NFL's relationship with the U.S. military came under scrutiny in a scandal over what became known as paid patriotism. A joint oversight report released by Arizona Republican Senators Jeff Flake and John McCain revealed that the U.S. Department of Defense (DoD) paid professional sports leagues almost $7 million to host events honoring the U.S. military. The NFL received the majority of that money, around $6 million. The practice was abruptly terminated by the league after fan criticism but left many with the idea that the NFL's growing embrace of the military and patriotism was a cynical ploy to appeal to conservative fans.

There was also controversy when NFL players began to protest real-life events. In August 2014, the shooting and killing of Michael Brown, an unarmed, 18-year-old African American man in Ferguson, Missouri, at the hands of Darren Wilson, a white police officer, set off a firestorm of violent protests. A few months later, five African American football players with the St. Louis Rams—Stedman Bailey, Tavon Austin, Jared Cook, Kenny Britt, and Chris Givens—gave a "hands up, don't shoot" gesture involving raised arms above the head in front of the crowd as they ran onto the field for pregame activities. The gesture had become an iconic part of the Ferguson demonstrations, representing Brown's alleged surrender to police immediately before he was shot. The five players were not penalized for this protest, but they faced a backlash from pro-police groups and conservative football commentators and fans who believed that NFL players should focus on football and not on protesting. When the NFL player protests during the national anthem began a few years later, concerns about police killings of African American men remained in the forefront.

Origins of the NFL Protest

Before Kaepernick began protesting in 2016, criminal justice experts had already widely acknowledged the huge racial disparities in the way U.S. law enforcement used force. A 2015 analysis of Federal Bureau of Investigation statistics showed that although African Americans comprised 13 percent of the population, they accounted for 31 percent of killings by police in 2012 (Lopez 2017). A 2015 study by *The Guardian* reported that young black men were nine times more likely than other Americans to be killed by police officers, despite making up only 2 percent of the U.S. population (Swaine et al. 2015). According to researchers, about one in every 65 deaths of young African American men in the United States is at the hands of police (Swaine et al. 2015).

Moreover, black people represent a disproportionately large percentage of the U.S. prison population, and they are more likely to be arrested for drug-related crimes, even though they are no more likely to use or sell drugs than the white community. Numerous studies with similar results led many criminal justice authorities to conclude that the racial disparities in both policing and criminal sentencing had a profound impact on both the black community and race relations in the United States.

In recent years, a series of high-profile killings of African American men spotlighted this racial disparity. In Florida, the 2012 killing of Trayvon Martin, a 17-year-old African American, attracted national attention. George Zimmerman, a neighborhood-watch volunteer, shot and killed Martin after confronting the young man as he walked home through his gated neighborhood. Zimmerman shot the unarmed Martin after the encounter turned physical. During his trial for Martin's murder, Zimmerman claimed self-defense, accusing Martin of attacking him to the point where he was afraid for his own life. In July 2013, a jury found Zimmerman not guilty of second-degree murder.

The Zimmerman verdict was polarizing. Many Americans agreed with the decision, arguing that Zimmerman had the right to defend himself in a physical encounter with Martin if he truly believed his life was in danger. However, many Americans, especially in the African American community, viewed the verdict as just another example of racism in criminal sentencing. The charge that a teenager in a hoodie had been racially profiled—confronted by Zimmerman for no reason other than his race—generated widespread outrage over the verdict, leading to the founding of Black Lives Matter, a civil rights movement involved in many social justice campaigns in recent years.

The Trayvon Martin case inspired many black athletes to speak out. In 2012, the NBA's Miami Heat posted a picture on social media of several players wearing hoodies with the hood up—the same way Martin had worn his on the night he was killed. They also wrote messages on their sneakers, such as "RIP Trayvon Martin" and "We want justice," which they then wore during televised games. For these African American athletes, Martin's death hit close to home. Many current and former NBA players used their social media platforms to urge action on criminal sentencing laws, particularly the controversial Florida "stand your ground" law that led to Zimmerman's acquittal.

Over the next few years, several incidents involving police killing African American men stoked the controversy. Eric Garner's death was one of the most controversial. On July 17, 2014, Garner died after being restrained in an illegal chokehold by a New York City police officer after a confrontation over selling individual cigarettes. A grand jury declined to indict the officer, Daniel Pantaleo, for Garner's killing.

Less than a month later, Darren Wilson, a white police officer in Ferguson, Missouri, shot and killed Michael Brown, a young, unarmed black man. Outrage over Brown's death led to demonstrations in Ferguson and Columbia, the home of the main campus of the University of Missouri. Escalating racial tensions at the university led to growing protests, culminating in a threat from the University of Missouri football team to go on strike until Tim Wolfe, the president of the university system, stepped down. Wolfe announced his resignation on November 9, 2015.

Finally, only a month before Colin Kaepernick's protests began, two police officers in Baton Rouge, Louisiana, shot and killed Alton Sterling, a 37-year-old black man, at close range. Later, the officers justified the shooting as self-defense, claiming they thought Sterling was reaching for a gun tucked in the waistband of his pants. Bystanders filmed the confrontation, and the video's broadcast sparked widespread calls for justice.

It is within the context of these tragic and deadly incidents that many people view Colin Kaepernick's actions on the football field in August 2016. As his protest drew media attention, Kaepernick made clear he felt it was time to make a stand. "I am not going to stand up to show pride in a flag for a country that oppresses black people and people of color," Kaepernick explained. "To me, this is bigger than football and it would be selfish on my part to look the other way. There are bodies on the street and people getting paid leave and getting away with murder" (Wyche 2016).

The Role of Political Partisanship

By September 2016, the form of Kaepernick's protests had evolved from sitting on the bench to taking a knee alongside his standing teammates during the national anthem. In the weeks that followed, a number of NFL players joined the #TakeAKnee demonstrations. Eric Reid, a teammate of Kaepernick's on the 49ers, was the first to kneel alongside him. On other NFL teams, there were players who also knelt or raised a fist in the air. Other players supported the protesters by placing a hand on a kneeling player's shoulder to signal solidarity. As the season came to an end, the protests continued to involve only a handful of players—many seemed to believe that the protests had met their goals.

Nevertheless, as the 2017–2018 season geared up, NFL protests remained a polarizing topic on sports talk radio and political shows on cable TV networks. Many supported the protests as an effective way to generate discussion about police brutality, racial inequality, and criminal justice reform. Critics, however, argued that taking a knee during the national anthem was disrespectful to the flag, the military, and the country.

At a political rally in Huntsville, Alabama, President Donald J. Trump jumped into the controversy on September 22, 2017, deriding the demonstrators as unpatriotic and disrespectful. In addition, he suggested NFL owners would be heroes if they fired any player who participated in the protests, saying, "Wouldn't you love to see one of these NFL owners, when somebody disrespects our flag, to say 'Get that son of a b**** off that field right now! Out! He's fired. He's fired!'" (Graham 2017).

Trump's insults garnered cheers from his supporters but also set off a firestorm of controversy. NFL owners, league officials, team personnel, and players rejected the president's rhetoric as divisive and counterproductive. In the following weeks, more players than ever protested, and those who did not participate signaled their solidarity with those who did.

Over many years, the NFL had crafted a conservative and patriotic image. The injection of partisan politics through high-profile protests turned many of Trump's Republican supporters against NFL football. Throughout the season, Trump continued to attack protesting players as unpatriotic, while also criticizing the league for allowing their perceived disrespect of the nation's military and its flag. The president's repeated sniping at the league took a toll by exacerbating the political divide around the issue. Many viewed his exploitation of the protests as just another a battle in his ongoing culture war and a surefire way to mobilize his base supporters as well as a deliberate strategy to distract from negative media coverage about his administration. Others regarded it as evidence of his racism.

Public opinion polls reflected the partisan divide. A May 2018 Morning Consult poll reported that 83 percent of Republicans opposed NFL players kneeling during the national anthem, while 43 percent of Independents and 25 percent of Democrats were against it (Sabin, 2018). Between September 2017 and May 2018, Republican opposition to the protests had increased from 77 percent to 83 percent, reflecting a much more polarized position than either Independents or Democrats (Sabin, 2018). There was also a partisan divide over how Trump treated black athletes in general. An August 2018 CBS/YouGov poll reported that 65 percent of Republicans approved of Trump's attitude toward black athletes who protested, while only 32 percent of all Americans approved of it (Salvanto, 2018). For league officials, public opinion polls underscored the threat to the league's long-term financial success. A new policy, top NFL officials and team owners came to believe, was necessary to get the focus off the controversy and back on the game of football.

Patriotism and American Values

After the 2016–2017 season, the NFL and team owners were ready to review and tighten the league's national anthem policy. On May 23, 2018, NFL owners introduced a new policy at the conclusion of their spring meetings. It required players and team personnel to stand if they were on the field during the anthem; however, it included an option for players and team personnel to stay in the locker room if they preferred. The league would have the option of fining individual team members found in violation of the policy.

Instead of resolving the controversy, the new policy was criticized by players, commentators, and fans as a violation of players' constitutional rights to free speech and an effort by the league to curb their social justice activism. These critics of the new policy argued that the players involved in the #TakeAKnee protests were exercising one of the most important constitutional rights, the right to free speech. Therefore, they said, NFL players should not be regarded as ungrateful and unpatriotic but rather should be celebrated for having the fortitude to confront racial and social injustice in spite of opposition from the president of the United States.

Many NFL fans, however, supported the league's new policy. They applauded the NFL's restrictions on the players' ability to protest on the field, arguing that they should not have the right to demonstrate during the playing of "The Star-Spangled Banner," a ritual symbolizing respectful appreciation for the United States of America and its ideals. Many fans expressed support for the players' social justice activism but criticized the timing and place of their actions. They urged players to stick to the game and reserve protests and activism for off the field. It was widely anticipated by league officials, team owners, and some fans that the new policy would facilitate a return to the game and reduce controversy on and off the field.

In response to these mixed reactions, in July 2018 the NFL put the new policy on hold. They announced that the NFL and the National Football League Players Association (NFLPA) would organize talks on how to more effectively address the issue of the #TakeAKnee protests.

In August 2018, TV network ESPN announced that it would no longer air the playing of "The Star-Spangled Banner" during its Monday Night Football broadcasts. CBS also confirmed that it would continue its policy of excluding the national anthem when broadcasting football games. Although the announcements drew criticism from President Trump, many regarded the networks' policies as an effective way of avoiding controversy and keeping the focus on the game itself.

That same month, a viral video caught the attention of hundreds of thousands of NFL fans. At a town hall meeting, Beto O'Rourke, a Democratic candidate for senate in Texas, gave a thoughtful response to a question about his position on the NFL protests. In the process, he reminded viewers of the original reasons for the demonstrations and the quintessentially American nature of protest itself.

"Peaceful, nonviolent protests, including taking a knee at a football game to point out that black men, unarmed, black teenagers, unarmed, and black children, unarmed, are being killed at a frightening level right now, including by members of law enforcement, without accountability and without justice," O'Rourke reminded the crowd. "And this problem—as grave as it is—is not going to fix itself and they're frustrated, frankly, with people like me, and those in positions of public trust and power who have been unable to resolve this or bring justice to what has been done, and to stop it from continuing to happen in this country. And so nonviolently, peacefully, while the eyes of this country are watching these games, they take a knee to bring our attention and our focus to this problem to ensure that we fix it. That is why they're doing it and I can think of nothing more American than to peacefully stand up or take a knee for your rights anytime, anywhere, any place" (@nowthisnews, August 21, 2018).

Further Reading

Graham, Bryan Armen. 2017. "Donald Trump Blasts NFL Anthem Protesters: 'Get That Son of a B**** off the Field'." *The Guardian*, September 23, 2017. https://www.theguardian.com/sport/2017/sep/22/donald-trump-nfl -national-anthem-protests

Lopez, German. 2017. "Police Shootings and Brutality in the US: 9 Things You Should Know." *Vox,* May 6, 2017. https://www.vox.com/cards/police -brutality-shootings-us/us-police-racism

NowThis (@nowthisnews). 2018. Twitter Post, August 21, 2018, 2:33 PM https:// twitter.com/nowthisnews/status/1032017750829531142?lang=en

Sabin, Sam. 2018. "NFL's National Anthem Policy Draws Support from 53% of U.S. Adults in Poll." *Morning Consult,* May 31, 2018. https://morning consult.com/2018/05/31/nfls-national-anthem-policy-draws-support-us -adults-poll/https://morningconsult.com/2018/05/31/nfls-national-anthem -policy-draws-support-us-adults-poll/

Salvanto, Anthony. 2018. "Poll: One Year after Charlottesville, Majority of Americans See Racial Tensions on the Rise." *CBS News,* August 12, 2018. https:// www.cbsnews.com/news/poll-one-year-after-charlottesville-americans-see -racial-tensions-on-increase/

Swaine, Jon, Oliver Laughland, Jamiles Lartey, and Ciara McCarthy. 2015. "Young Black Men Killed by Police at Highest Rate in Year of 1,134 Deaths." *The Guardian,* December 31, 2015. https://www.theguardian.com/us-news/ 2015/dec/31/the-counted-police-killings-2015-young-black-men

Wyche, Steve. 2016. "Colin Kaepernick Explains Why He Sat during National Anthem." NFL.com, August 28, 2016. http://www.nfl.com/news/story/ 0ap3000000691077/article/colin-kaepernick-explains-protest-of-national -anthem

CHAPTER TWO

Landmark Events

This section explores important milestones in the evolution of the recent protests by National Football League players, from the first time "The Star-Spangled Banner" was played at a sporting event in 1918, to protests against racism by African American athletes in the mid-twentieth century, to Colin Kaepernick's decision to kneel during the National Anthem in 2016 and its aftermath.

"The Star-Spangled Banner" Is Played at a Sporting Event for the First Time (1918)

During the late nineteenth century, the rise of organized sports leagues provided opportunities for Americans from all walks of life to come together and enjoy the spectacle of uniquely American pastimes such as baseball, basketball, and football. Sports events helped newcomers assimilate. Immigrants arriving in the United States were able to participate in American customs and cultural experiences and meet other residents from different socioeconomic and cultural backgrounds while finding common ground in their support of a local sports team.

The introduction of patriotic songs before games was another unifying element for these often diverse crowds. Whatever their backgrounds, fans came together to sing patriotic songs and celebrate being Americans.

The Rise of "The Star-Spangled Banner"

According to scholar Mark Ferris, the earliest documented performance of "The Star-Spangled Banner" at a U.S. baseball game occurred on May 15, 1862, at a match held at Union Base Ball and Cricket Grounds in Brooklyn, New York (Ferris 2014). Playing "The Star-Spangled Banner" was thought especially appropriate because the country was fighting the Civil War. Written in 1814 by Francis Scott Key, the patriotic song had become a favorite with many Americans, who were inspired by Key's lyrics chronicling an American naval victory against the British.

The song's popularity received another boost during World War I, when it was often performed at patriotic events. In 1916, President Woodrow Wilson designated the song as the informal anthem of the U.S. military and ordered it played at military celebrations and ceremonies. Two years later, Representative John Linthicum (D-MD) proposed a bill to designate "The Star-Spangled Banner" the official national anthem, but he failed to get the votes in Congress to pass it. In the view of many Americans, however, the song was already the national anthem of the United States.

The 1918 World Series

On September 5, 1918, the Chicago Cubs and the Boston Red Sox were scheduled to compete in the World Series in Chicago, Illinois. In the weeks leading up to the series, however, city lawmakers and baseball officials debated whether the World Series should proceed in light of the large number of military fatalities and injuries the United States was experiencing in World War I. In the months since the United States entered the war in April 1917, some 100,000 American soldiers had died. The minds of many fans were on the conflict raging overseas and baseball did not seem important in the shadow of war. When it was reported that U.S. troops stationed in Europe were looking forward to the competition, officials decided to hold the games as scheduled.

On the eve of the World Series, someone tossed a bomb into the entrance of the Chicago Federal Building in downtown Chicago, killing four people and injuring dozens more. The bombing set the city on edge and inspired concern that the game could be the target of an attack. As a result, the crowd at the opening game of the series was smaller than usual; in fact, only about 20,000 fans showed up at the ballpark for the event. The crowd was also uncharacteristically restrained. "For a baseball game in a world's championship series, yesterday's combat between the Cubs and Red Sox was perhaps the quietest on record," reported the *Chicago Tribune* (quoted in Cypher and Trex 2011).

The small crowd witnessed a close game. Babe Ruth, one of baseball's truly legendary players, was pitching a shutout, which means not allowing a run, for the Red Sox going into the seventh-inning stretch. During the break, a 12-piece band from the Great Lakes Naval Training center north of Chicago broke into a rousing rendition of "The Star-Spangled Banner" to honor American troops.

Fred Thomas, Red Sox third baseman, had been granted a furlough from the Navy so he could play in the World Series. When he heard the song begin, he turned toward the flag and gave a military salute. His teammates on the field followed his lead and gave a civilian salute, putting their hands over their hearts. The crowd came alive for the first time during the game, cheering and singing along to the band's performance.

According to a report in the *New York Times,* the music inspired a groundswell of patriotism in the crowd. "The yawn was checked and heads were bared as ball players turned quickly about and faced the music," the article stated. "First the song was taken up by a few, then others joined, and when the final notes came, a great volume of melody rolled across the field. It was at the very end that the onlookers exploded into thunderous applause and rent the air with a cheer that marked the highest point of today's enthusiasm" (*New York Times* 1918). The Red Sox went on to win the game 1-0.

Cubs officials hoped to repeat the enthusiastic crowd response during the next few games, arranging for "The Star-Spangled Banner" to be played once again during the seventh-inning stretch by the Great Lakes Naval Training Center band. As in the first game, the performance was a huge hit with fans. Word got out, and the series unfolded without any further violence. Fan attendance surged at later games played in Chicago.

Red Sox officials took note and scheduled a local band to play the anthem during the pregame festivities at Fenway Park in Boston. In addition, the team gave away free tickets to wounded World War I veterans. According to the *Chicago Tribune,* the entrance of the war heroes onto the field before the sixth game of the series inspired a strong reaction from the fans: "their entrance on crutches supported by their comrades evoked louder cheers than anything the athletes did on the diamond" (Cypher and Trex 2011).

Further Reading

Babwin, Don. 2017. "1918 World Series Started the U.S. Love Affair with the National Anthem." *Chicago Tribune*, July 3, 2017. http://www .chicagotribune.com/sports/baseball/ct-wrigley-field-national-anthem -20170703-story.html#

Cyphers, Luke, and Ethan Trex. 2011. "The Song Remains the Same." *ESPN The Magazine*, September 19, 2011. http://www.espn.com/espn/story/_/id/ 6957582/the-history-national-anthem-sports-espn-magazine

Ferris, Marc. 2014. *Star-Spangled Banner: The Unlikely Story of America's National Anthem.* Baltimore: Johns Hopkins University Press.

New York Times Company. 1918. "Red Sox Beat Cubs in Initial Battle of World Series." *New York Times*, September 6, 1918. https://timesmachine.nytimes.com/timesmachine/1918/09/06/97025138.pdf

Thorn, John. 2017. "The Star-Spangled Banner." *Our Game*, May 23, 2017. https://ourgame.mlblogs.com/the-star-spangled-banner-2689d0a030e4

The United States World War I Centennial Commission. 2018. "The Star Spangled Banner and World War One." www.worldwar1centennial.org, 2018. https://www.worldwar1centennial.org/index.php/educate/places/the-star-spangled-banner-and-world-war-one.html

Waxman, Olivia. 2017. "Here's How Standing for the National Anthem Became Part of U.S. Sports Tradition." *Time*, September 25, 2017. http://time.com/4955623/history-national-anthem-sports-nfl/

"The Star-Spangled Banner" Becomes the National Anthem (1931)

Although there was no official national anthem in the United States throughout the nineteenth century, a number of patriotic and popular tunes functioned informally in that role. One such song was "America the Beautiful," written by Katherine Lee Bates, an English teacher who wrote it after climbing Colorado's Pike's Peak, inspired by the area's natural beauty. An early ditty from the eighteenth century, "Yankee Doodle Dandy," initially featured lyrics written by Dr. Richard Shuckburgh, a British army surgeon, to mock colonial troops during the pre-Revolutionary War period, but American soldiers proudly adopted the tune to taunt the British, performing it at parades and political rallies. Another patriotic song played frequently at public events was "My Country 'Tis of Thee," a song written by Reverend Samuel Francis Smith in 1831. Another song, with lyrics written by Julia Ward Howe, "The Battle Hymn of the Republic" (1861), was prevalent as a Union rallying song during the Civil War, which made the song divisive in the South even long after the war ended.

Francis Scott Key's "The Star-Spangled Banner" (1814) was also a favorite patriotic tune during the nineteenth century. It was a popular song for rallies and holiday parties during the Civil War and World War I and gradually came to be considered the informal anthem of the U.S. military. In 1916, President Woodrow Wilson ordered that the song be played during official military events. When the American public turned its attention to choosing an official anthem for the nation, "The Star-Spangled Banner" seemed to be a good candidate.

Introduction of National Anthem Legislation

The first attempt to name "The Star-Spangled Banner" as the official national anthem of the United States can be traced back to April 10, 1918, when Representative John Linthicum (D-MD) introduced a bill to do just that. Congress did not pass the bill, however, and did not consider the issue again for a number of years.

On April 15, 1929, Linthicum tried again. He introduced H.R. 14, also known as An Act to Make The Star-Spangled Banner the National Anthem of the United States, to Congress. The bill read: "Be it enacted by the Senate and House of Representatives of the United States of America in Congress assembled, that the composition consisting of the words and music known as The Star Spangled Banner is designated the national anthem of the United States of America" (National Archives 2018).

The bill then went to the House Judiciary Committee, which put off scheduling a hearing until almost a year later. As the hearing finally drew near, Linthicum urged his fellow lawmakers to support the measure. "This country needs a national song to give expression to its patriotism," he argued (quoted in Glass 2010). He also submitted a petition with more than five million signatures in support of the bill as well as numerous telegrams urging the passage of the measure from many of the nation's governors and key business and civic leaders.

Linthicum's campaign was boosted by the popular syndicated comic strip, *Ripley's Believe It or Not!* On November 3, 1929, cartoonist Robert Ripley published a comic strip reminding readers: "Believe it or not, America has no national anthem." Many disbelieving Americans wrote angry letters to Ripley, who urged them to write their congressional representatives to complain. Scholars believe that Ripley's efforts greatly aided Linthicum's campaign to recruit American citizens to his cause.

The Anthem Debate

One of the main criticisms of the bill was that "The Star-Spangled Banner" was too difficult to sing. Detractors claimed that the song's range was too wide and its pitch too high, making it difficult for bass and alto singers to reach the high notes and tenors and sopranos to reach the low ones. These critics argued that the national anthem should at least be easy to sing.

Other arguments were leveled against "The Star-Spangled Banner." Prohibitionists maintained that the song was basically a poem set to the music of a rowdy English drinking song, "To Anachreon in Heaven," making it inappropriate for formal patriotic occasions. Others considered the tune, which chronicles the bloody battle against British naval forces for Fort McHenry in Baltimore Harbor during the War of 1812, as an insult to England, which had been a staunch American ally during World War I. Furthermore, critics said the lyrics were too violent, making the song an unsuitable anthem for schoolchildren. The song was also perceived as essentially foreign in nature because its melody was a British tune.

Representative Linthicum's motives came under scrutiny as well. The Maryland legislator's district encompassed most of the city of Baltimore, where the 1814 events that had inspired Francis Scott Key's original poem took place. To some observers, Linthicum's efforts to make "The Star-Spangled Banner" the national anthem seemed to promote Baltimore rather than patriotic pride.

During the hearing in February 1930, supporters of H.R. 14 brought in the U.S. Navy Band and two sopranos to perform "The Star-Spangled Banner" before the committee. They hoped to show the legislators how easy the song was to sing, thereby convincing them to vote for the bill. The stunt went over well with Congress, increasing goodwill toward the measure.

The campaign also received a boost from the words of prominent composer John Philip Sousa. Although he reportedly favored a homegrown anthem, Sousa argued that Key's lyrics were "soul-stirring." In addition, Sousa commented, "it is the spirit of the music that inspires" (quoted in the Library of Congress 2002). Sousa had led performances of his own version of the tune while touring Europe. According to Mark Hildebrand, the director behind the 2012 documentary *Anthem—The Story behind "The Star-Spangled Banner,"* Sousa "slowed it down, made it more majestic. Its original pace, as indicated on the sheet music, was 'con spirito' [in a lively manner]. It was meant to be fast-paced, bouncy" (quoted in Ng 2016). For many Americans, Sousa's arrangement gave the tune the gravitas expected of a patriotic anthem.

On April 21, 1930, the House of Representatives passed Linthicum's bill. The Senate approved the bill on March 3, 1931, as one of the final acts of the 71st Congress. The next day, President Herbert Hoover signed the bill into law.

However, the new law did not designate an official text or musical arrangement as the official version of the anthem. As a result, various creative arrangements and interpretations of the song, from traditional to unconventional, were performed over the years. Famous composers, like Sousa and John Williams, have created their own arrangements of the piece, while pop stars including Jimmy Hendrix, Whitney Houston, Jose Feliciano, and Fergie have performed creative and memorable interpretations of their own.

Further Reading

Cavanaugh, Ray. 2016. "The Star-Spangled Banner: An American Anthem with a Very British Beginning." *The Guardian*, July 4, 2016. https://www .theguardian.com/music/2016/jul/04/star-spangled-banner-national -anthem-british-origins

Dunn, Catherine. 2016. "Five Songs That Were Almost the Anthem." Townhall.com, September 16, 2016. https://townhall.com/tipsheet/catheri nedunn/2016/09/16/five-songs-that-were-almost-the-national-anthem -n2218303

Glass, Andrew. 2010. " 'Star-Spangled Banner' Becomes Official U.S. Anthem." *Politico*, March 3, 2010. https://www.politico.com/story/2010/03/star -spangled-banner-becomes-official-us-anthem-march-3-1931-033775

Library of Congress. 2002. "Star Spangled Banner." https://loc.gov/item/ ihas.200000017

National Archives and Records Administration. 2018. H.R. 14, An Act to Make The Star Spangled Banner the National Anthem of the United States of America, April 21, 1930. https://www.visitthecapitol.gov/exhibitions/artifact/hr-14 -act-make-star-spangled-banner-national-anthem-united-states-america-0

Ng, David. 2016. "How 'The Star-Spangled Banner,' Racist or Not, Became Our National Anthem." *Los Angeles Times*, September 6, 2016. http:// www.latimes.com/entertainment/arts/la-et-cm-star-spangled-banner -racism-20160823-snap-story.html

The NFL Mandates the National Anthem Be Played before Games (1945)

During World War II, displays of patriotism in the United States were a vital part of the nation's war efforts on the battlefield and at home. For those on the home front, it was essential to convey to American troops fighting overseas that their fellow Americans supported their heroic efforts. It also united the American people behind a common purpose, facilitating the assimilation of immigrants and people of different backgrounds into American society and helping to shape a proud American identity. Symbols of patriotism, such as the flag and the national anthem, were crucial to that effort.

With that in mind, Congress formed the National Anthem Committee to establish a policy, known as "The Code for the National Anthem of the United States," to oversee the playing of the national anthem in a public setting. For example, the code established the tradition of the audience standing and singing "The Star-Spangled Banner." The code states, "[s]ince the message of the Anthem is carried largely in the text, it is essential that emphasis be place upon the *singing* of the Star Spangled Banner. . . . On all occasions the group singing the National Anthem should stand facing the flag or the leader, in an attitude of respectful attention. Outdoors, men should remove their hats" (*NAC* 1942).

The National Football League and the National Anthem

The NFL adopted the practice of playing "The Star-Spangled Banner" before every game during the 1941–1942 season as a display of patriotism and support for U.S. soldiers fighting in World War II. Over the next few years, the practice continued in the NFL as well as in other professional sports leagues. The ritual proved to be a popular part of the pregame activities, often following the introduction of wounded war veterans, the commemoration of the fallen, or the celebration of military victories. During those years, the nation became accustomed to patriotic displays before baseball games, football games, and other sporting events.

When the war ended in 1945, the National Football League mandated that the practice of playing "The Star-Spangled Banner" before every game continue. The league viewed it not only as a moment of rousing entertainment, but as a patriotic way to bring fans, players, and officials together before the game. As NFL Commissioner Elmer Layden observed, "The playing of the national anthem should be as much a part of every game as the kickoff. We must not drop it simply because the war is over. We should never forget what it stands for" (Willingham 2017).

The Role of Technology

Improved technology was a key factor in popularizing the national anthem. During the early twentieth century, it was hard to effectively broadcast and amplify sound for large stadium crowds. Early on, the only sound systems available were basic public address systems, and they were only used to make public service announcements. In order for crowds to hear the anthem at all, teams had to hire local bands—often large military bands—to perform the anthem live on the field. Most teams could only afford to do this on special occasions, like an opening day event or a playoff game.

As technology advanced in the years after World War II, larger and more powerful sound systems were installed in stadiums. This not only helped the audience hear and participate but also allowed for the use of recordings of the national anthem, eliminating the expense of hiring a live band.

As popular music shifted from big bands and crooners to pop stars, increasingly powerful and reliable stadium sound systems allowed individual singers and musicians as well as small musical groups to perform "The Star-Spangled Banner" in front of thousands of fans, a feat that would not have been possible in the nineteenth or early twentieth centuries. Performers often brought their own interpretations or arrangements to the song. Although this sometimes made for controversial renditions of the national anthem, like Roseanne Barr's 1990 infamous version, it also led to innovative and talked-about performances that kept the anthem relevant and interesting to contemporary audiences.

The NFL's National Anthem Policy

When NFL Commissioner Elmer Layden mandated that his league continue to include a performance of the national anthem before every football game, he established a custom that every NFL team followed year after year. Yet it was not a league rule.

In 1978, however, the NFL formally established the policy in the league's game operations manual, a collection of more than 200 procedures and policies dictating the conditions under which games should be played. For example, the manual describes the number and type of medical personnel required for each game and the type of communications equipment each team can use during a game. According to the NFL, "The league's Game Operations Department uses the manual to govern the conduct of home clubs, to ensure that they protect players and provide the conditions for a fair and fan-friendly contest. Clubs face warnings and other penalties for noncompliance" (NFL 2018).

The policy regarding the national anthem in the game operations manual dictates the following: "The National Anthem must be played prior to every NFL game, and all players must be on the sideline for the National Anthem. During the National Anthem, players on the field and bench area should stand at attention, faced the flag, hold helmets in their left hand, and refrain from talking" (NFL 2018).

Therefore, every NFL team followed the policy of playing the national anthem before every game. If players were on the field, they were required to be on the sideline; in practice, though, the league allowed players to stay in the locker rooms during pregame festivities for many primetime broadcasts, such as *Monday Night Football*. It wasn't until 2009 that the NFL addressed the inconsistency of the policy and required players to be on the field for pregame events for all scheduled games.

Further Reading

Fitzpatrick, Alex. 2017. "Does the NFL Require Players to Stand for the National Anthem?" *Time*, September 25, 2017. http://time.com/4955704/nfl-league -rulebook-a62-63-national-anthem-rule/

National Anthem Committee. 1942. "The Code for the National Anthem of the United States of America." *Bulletin of the Music Teachers National Association*, vol. 7, no. 2, December 1942. https://www.jstor.org/stable/43528494? seq=1#page_scan_tab_contents

National Football League. 2018. "League Governance." https://operations.nfl.com/ football-ops/league-governance/

Willingham, A. J. 2017. "The National Anthem in Sports (Spoiler: It Wasn't Always This Way)." CNN, September 25, 2017. https://www.cnn.com/2017/09/25/ us/nfl-national-anthem-trump-kaepernick-history-trnd/index.html

Smith and Carlos Give the Black Power Salute at the Olympic Games (1968)

An iconic moment of social justice activism in the history of sports occurred when two black athletes from the United States, Tommie Smith and John Carlos, raised their fists in a black power salute while receiving their medals at the 1968 Summer Olympics in Mexico City. This act of defiance, coming at the end of a summer of racial unrest and growing demonstrations against the Vietnam War, led to widespread condemnation of Smith and Carlos for violating the apolitical spirit of the Olympic Games. The impact of that single powerful action by these two world-class athletes spread across the world. The gesture has come to symbolize the influence that individual political protest can bring to bear on the global conversation about inequality, poverty, and world peace.

The Context for the Protest

The 1968 Summer Olympics were held in October, after a summer of politically charged violence and racial unrest. The event took place only months after the assassination of civil rights leader Martin Luther King Jr., who was shot and killed by a white man, James Earl Ray, in Memphis, Tennessee. In June, Democratic presidential candidate Robert F. Kennedy was killed by an assassin's bullet while campaigning in Los Angeles.

Racial tensions erupted into riots in several major U.S. cities, including Baltimore, Kansas City, Chicago, and Washington, D.C. In late August 1968, political demonstrations exploded into bloody conflict at the Democratic National Convention in Chicago, where police clashed violently with thousands of anti-Vietnam War demonstrators. Scenes of the chaos were broadcast all over the world.

As African American men, both John Carlos and Tommie Smith were informed by both the civil rights and black power movements of the 1960s. The civil rights movement was a struggle for social justice using nonviolent protest during the 1950s and 1960s. Its goals were to end institutionalized racial segregation and discrimination and attain racial equality under federal, state, and local laws. The black power movement focused on fostering racial pride, artistic and cultural achievement, and economic empowerment in the black community in the United States.

As students at San Jose University, Smith and Carlos were active in the struggle for civil rights and black empowerment. Both men helped found the Olympic Project for Human Rights, a social justice organization formed in 1968 to combat racism in sports. The organization advocated a boycott of the 1968 Olympics unless four conditions were met: the withdrawal of Olympic invitations for both South Africa and Rhodesia (two African countries ruled through a racial apartheid system); the return of Muhammad Ali's heavyweight boxing title, stripped from him because of his religious objections to fighting in the Vietnam War; the hiring of more African American coaches; and the firing of Avery Brundage, the head of the International Olympic Committee and a known white supremacist and Nazi sympathizer.

In compliance with one of these demands, the IOC withdrew its invitation to Rhodesia and South Africa. However, they failed to meet the other demands. Despite that outcome, Smith and Carlos decided to attend the games, hoping that their participation would raise awareness of social justice issues and give them an opportunity to protest on the world stage.

Ten days before the games were set to begin, Mexican government troops massacred student activists gathered at Three Cultures Square in Mexico City. An estimated 300 to 400 young people were killed.

The 1968 Summer Olympics

Tommie Smith and John Carlos were elite track-and-field athletes. As a student at San Jose University, Smith set National Collegiate Athletic Association records in the 200 meters and 220 yard races and won the association's Men's Outdoor Track and Field Championship in 1966. Carlos was Smith's teammate at San Jose University and had beaten Smith in the 200 meter dash. Both athletes were world-class sprinters competing in the 200 meter dash in Mexico City.

On October 15, 1969, the finals of the 200 meter dash event were held in Olympic Stadium. Tommie Smith won the gold medal with a time of 20:83, setting a new world record. Australian sprinter Peter Norman came in second with a time of 20:06, earning him the silver medal. John Carlos grabbed the bronze medal with a third-place time of 20:10.

As the medal ceremony approached, Carlos and Smith readied themselves for a protest on the podium. Smith donned a black scarf to symbolize black pride, while Carlos put on a beaded necklace in memory of all the black men and women who had been lynched in the United States. As a gesture of solidarity with the working class, Carlos unzipped his track suit. He had forgotten his black gloves, so Smith had given him his left-handed glove. All three medal winners—Smith, Norman, and Carlos—wore an Olympic Project for Human Rights patch on their jackets. As the two men walked to the podium, they took off their shoes to protest black poverty.

After the medals were given out to Smith, Normal, and Carlos on the podium, the U.S. national anthem began to play. Both men bowed their heads, then Smith raised his right fist into the air while Carlos raised his left. The American photographer and photojournalist John Dominis took a picture that became iconic.

Carlos recalled, "As the anthem began and the crowd saw us raise our fists, the stadium became eerily quiet. For a few seconds, you could have heard a frog p*** on cotton. There's something awful about hearing fifty thousand people go silent, like being in the eye of a hurricane" (Brown 2017).

Aftermath

Within hours, the IOC called for the suspension of Smith and Carlos from the U.S. Olympic Team and their removal from the Olympic Village, the area where Olympic athletes were housed during the games, for violating Olympic rules by making a political statement. When the U.S. Olympic Committee refused to comply, the IOC threatened to suspend the entire track-and-field team. So the U.S. Olympic Committee sent Smith and Carlos home.

In the United States, Tommie Smith and John Carlos were met with insults and death threats. They were suspended from the U.S. track team and largely ostracized by the track-and-field establishment. However, for many athletes, activists, and fans, Smith and Carlos had shown courage and provided a model for how athletes could impact social justice and raise awareness.

Reflecting on his actions years later, Tommie Smith maintained that the protest "represented a holistic idea of life, a holistic experience of equal rights, and that was in the back of my mind when the fist went to the sky in jubilation: a cry for freedom or a cry for hope. All of this was a culmination of the work that had gone in: the love, the experience of the academic experience, the experience of training physically and the jubilation of my doing what needed to be done."

"But it was done because I had no choice," he concluded. "To me it was a responsibility that I didn't want to do, but I had to do it because I was the only one at that particular time who could do it standing from that particular platform" (Martin and Whitney 2016).

Further Reading

Brown, DeNeen L. 2017. "They Didn't #TakeTheKnee: The Black Power Protest Salute That Shook the World in 1968." *The Washington Post*, September 24, 2017. https://www.washingtonpost.com/news/retropolis/wp/2017/09/24/they-didnt-takeaknee-the-black-power-protest-salute-that-shook-the-world-in-1968/?utm_term=.0a5cad186429

Martin, Jill, and Alvin Whitney. 2016. "Tommie Smith Reflects on Winning Gold, Iconic Salute Nearly 50 Years Later." CNN, August 18, 2016. https://www.cnn.com/2016/08/18/sport/tommie-smith-1968-olympic-games-reflection/index.html

Younge, Gary. 2012. "The Man Who Raised a Black Power Salute at the 1968 Olympic Games." *The Guardian*, March 30, 2012. https://www.theguardian.com/world/2012/mar/30/black-power-salute-1968-olympics

Zirin, Dave. 2008. "The Explosive 1968 Olympics." *International Socialist Review*, no. 61, September-October 2008. http://www.isreview.org/issues/61/feat-zirin.shtml

Zirin, Dave and Gareth Edwards. 2012. "Resistance: The Best Olympic Spirit." *International Socialism*, no. 135, June 28, 2012. http://isj.org.uk/resistance-the-best-olympic-spirit/

The Olympic Games Protest (1972)

Four years after Tommie Smith and John Carlos sparked controversy by raising their clenched fists at the 1968 Summer Olympic Games, another pair of American track-and-field stars made waves with a similar political statement. Vince Matthews and Wayne Collett drew widespread condemnation for their behavior, which included breaking protocol by standing together, refusing to pay attention, and raising their arms during the playing of the U.S. national anthem. As a result, the International Olympic Committee banned both athletes from Olympic competition for life. Their protests revived the debate about the role of political protest at the Olympic Games and in sports overall.

The Road to the 1972 Olympic Games

Going into the 1972 Olympic Games, the U.S. men's track-and-field team was an elite group of athletes expected to dominate many of the track events—and Vince Matthews and Wayne Collett were two of the team's finest long sprinters. Matthews won a gold medal for the 4 x 400 meter relay team at the 1968 Mexico City Olympic Games. Collett won the 400 meter at the U.S. Olympic Trials in 1972. The two athletes, along with teammate John Smith, were expected to compete for the top medals in the 400 meter sprint event.

On September 7, 1972, the 400 meter finals were held at Olympic Stadium in Munich, West Germany. Smith jumped ahead of the pack but pulled up with an injury, allowing Matthews to take the lead. Matthews won the gold with a time of 44.66, while Collett earned the silver with a time of 44.80.

The Medal Ceremony

After the event, Matthews and Collett took their positions on the podium and accepted their medals. The ceremony seemed to proceed in a conventional manner. Then the first notes of "The Star-Spangled Banner" began to play. That was when the behavior of the two athletes became controversial to IOC officials as well as to many fans in the stadium and around the world.

"Collett, bare-footed, leaped from the No. 2 tier to the No. 1 to stand beside his teammate," a reporter chronicled. "They stood sideways to the flag, twirling their medals, with Matthews stroking his chin. Their shoulders slumped, neither stood erect nor looked at the flag. Matthews raised both arms over his head as leaped off the stand. As whistles and catcalls continued, Collett raised a clenched fist to the crowd before entering the portal of the dressing room" (Associated Press 1972).

Even before the national anthem ended, German fans in the stands started a cacophony of loud whistling, a sign of disapproval. The many Americans in the stands reacted with heckles and catcalls directed at the two athletes.

Controversy Erupts

At first, Matthews denied that the two men engaged in any sort of political protest. "If we wanted to protest, we would do a better job than that," he said. "People are always trying to make something out of nothing. The reason Collett came on the stand with me was not a protest.... Collett stepped up to show that we are a team" (Associated Press 1972).

He argued that the crowd misinterpreted their actions on the podium. "It was kind of weird that the crowd tried to get some sort of symbolism from it. We came up with no protest in mind, but the crowd had protest in mind when we left" (Johnson 1972). Matthews also suggested their behavior on the podium stemmed from a beef with the team's coaching staff, not any political statement.

Collett, however, expressed different feelings in a radio interview with San Francisco reporter Sam Skinner shortly after the protest. "For maybe six or seven years, I've stood at attention while the anthem has been played, but I just can't do it with a clear conscience anymore the way things are in our country," he said. "There are a lot of things wrong, and I think maybe the white establishment has too casual an attitude with the blacks of America. They're not concerned unless we make a little noise and embarrass them" (quoted in Noland, 2010).

Much later, Collett maintained the protest should be understood within the context of civil rights struggles during the late 1960s and early 1970s. "I love America," he said. "I just don't think it's lived up to its promise. I'm not anti-American at all. To suggest otherwise is not to understand the struggle of blacks in America at the time" (quoted in Noland 2010).

Legacy

IOC head Avery Brundage called an emergency session of the executive board to deal with the emerging controversy over the incident. After the meeting, the IOC announced that Matthews and Collett would be allowed to keep their medals, but they were ordered to leave the Olympic Village and were banned from further Olympic competition.

In a letter to Buck, Brundage criticized the "disgusting display of your two athletes" and reminded him of the controversy surrounding the medal ceremony for Tommie Smith and John Carlos at the 1968 Olympics (Large 2012). He warned Buck that if another political protest took place, medals would be stripped from all participating athletes.

The USOC also imposed penalties on Matthews and Collett. In a letter to the two men, Buck outlined the additional punishment: "After careful consideration, it is the opinion of the USOC officers that because of your demonstrated flagrant disrespect for the flag of your country, and because of the discredit you have brought to our U.S. Olympic team, you are no longer eligible to wear any insignia of the 1972 USA Olympic Team. Accordingly, you will remove all patches and insignia from your clothing and competitive apparel" (Large 2012).

Despite the criticism of Matthews and Collett, there was also an understanding that elite athletes were complex people with a variety of interests and beliefs. Bill Bowerman, the legendary coach of the U.S. Olympic track team, observed, "You cannot expect on an Olympic squad of sixty to have everybody act like Army privates. They're great athletes. They're great individuals. The fact that some of them did things that the press objected to didn't bother me too much. They're vivid, alive, human animals. They're keenly interested, very competitive, and all different. So why not accept that and enjoy it?" (Large 2012).

Further Reading

Associated Press. 1972. "Milburn, Matthews Win Gold, but U.S. Trails." *Sarasota Herald-Tribune,* September 8, 1972. https://news.google.com/newspapers?id=gpwcAAAAIBAJ&sjid=mWYEAAAAIBAJ&pg=5359,2754393&dq=wayne+collett&hl=en

Johnson, Chuck. 1972. "Matthews, Collett Barred for Conduct on Victory Stand." *The Milwaukee Journal*, September 8, 1972. https://news.google.com/newspapers?id=cMAdAAAAIBAJ&sjid=oygEAAAAIBAJ&pg=7196,4127118&dq=wayne+collett&hl=en

Large, David Clay. 2012. *Munich 1972: Tragedy, Terror, and Triumph at the Olympic Games.* Rowman & Littlefield Publishers.

Noland, Claire. 2010. "Wayne Collett Dies at 60; UCLA Sprinter Won Silver Medal at '72 Olympics." *Los Angeles Times*, March 17, 2010. http://articles.latimes.com/2010/mar/17/local/la-me-wayne-collett18-2010mar18

Werner, Barry. 2016. "Colin Kaepernick's Protest at the Intersection of Patriotism and Athletics Is Far from New." Fox Sports, October 20, 2016. https://www.foxsports.com/nfl/story/colin-kaepernicks-protest-at-the-intersection-of-patriotism-and-athletics-is-far-from-new-083116

The NBA Suspends Mahmoud Abdul-Rauf for Not Standing during the Anthem (1996)

During the 1995–1996 season of the National Basketball Association (NBA), Denver Nuggets guard Mahmoud Abdul-Rauf chose not to stand and salute the American flag during the national anthem before each game. Instead, he did stretching exercises on the bench or stood with his hands on his hips, head lowered. Sometimes, he chose to remain in the locker room during the "The Star-Spangled Banner."

For months, Abdul-Rauf's quiet protest went unnoticed by media and most fans. In March, a local reporter mentioned it in an article. The next day, media requests for access to the team's practice session tripled. The national media began to focus on Abdul-Rauf's protest, which generated outrage from political figures, fans, and sports talk radio. Within hours, it was one of the most talked-about issues in sports.

On March 12, 1996, the NBA suspended Abdul-Rauf for one game. The league cited his violation of NBA rules as the reason.

The NBA's National Anthem Policy

According to the NBA's official rulebook, "Players, coaches, and trainers are to stand and line up in a dignified posture on the sidelines or on the foul line during the playing of the national anthem" (Seifert 2018). At the time, Russ Granik, then the league's deputy commissioner, said that there were no exceptions to the league's rule. "The NBA's rule on this point is very clear and all our rules apply to all players" (Hodges 1996).

The Origins of Abdul-Rauf's Protest

Abdul-Rauf's protest can be traced to his strong religious and social justice beliefs. Born Chris Jackson in Gulfport, Mississippi, Abdul-Rauf struggled with poverty as well as Tourette's syndrome, a condition characterized by motor and vocal tics, during his childhood. He excelled at basketball, which led to a college scholarship with Louisiana State University. After signing on as a professional basketball player with the Denver Nuggets, Abdul-Rauf converted to Islam and changed his name. Later, he cited his devotion to Islamic religious beliefs as central to his protest of the American flag.

The flag is "a symbol of oppression, of tyranny," he said to reporters around the time of his suspension. "This country has a long history of that. I don't think you can argue the facts. You can't be for God and for oppression. It's clear in the Koran, Islam is the only way. I don't criticize those who stand, so don't criticize me for sitting. I won't waver from my decision" (Hodges 1996).

In a later interview, Abdul-Rauf backed off from his condemnation of the flag, clarifying that it represented many things, some of which were positive. "I'm able to make a lot of money in the United States," he explained. "I'm from here and I'm not saying, again, that it represents everything bad.

I never said that. I'm just saying that it also represents the bad" (Hodges 1996).

He also maintained that his concern was rooted in more than his Muslim beliefs, stating "I just don't look at the United States, I just don't look at the Muslim issue. I look at the Caucasian Americans and I look at the African American being oppressed in this country and I don't stand for that" (Hodges 1996).

Aftermath

It was estimated that Abdul-Rauf's protest would cost him $31,707 a game. On March 13, he served his one-game suspension by sitting out the Nuggets game against the Orlando Magic. The next day, Abdul-Rauf and then NBA Commissioner David Stern reached a compromise: Abdul-Rauf had to stand with his body turned toward the flag during the playing of the national anthem, but he could bow his head and close his eyes. Abdul-Rauf decided to say a silent prayer during that time. Once both parties agreed to the compromise, Abdul-Rauf was allowed to resume play with his team.

He finished the season with a team high of 19.2 points and 6.8 assists per game. Despite his successful season on the basketball court, the Nuggets traded him to the Sacramento Kings. On his new team, his playing time dropped and he lost his starting position. In his view, he was pushed out. "They begin to try and put you in vulnerable positions," Abdul-Rauf recalled. "They play with your minutes, trying to mess up your rhythm. Then they sit you more. Then what it looks like is, well, the guy just doesn't have it anymore, so we trade him" (Washington 2016). When his contract with the Kings expired in 1998, no NBA team gave him a tryout.

Abdul-Rauf contends that his social justice activism and religious beliefs were to blame for his lack of NBA offers. "It's kind of like a setup," he maintained. "You know, trying to set you up to fail and so when they get rid of you, they can blame it on that as opposed to, it was really because he took those positions. They don't want these types of examples to spread, so they've got to make examples of individuals like this" (Washington 2016).

In 1998 Abdul-Rauf signed a two-year contract with a professional team in the Turkish Basketball League. Within months, however, he left the team, attributing his decision to a lack of interest in the game. He announced his retirement from basketball. However, in 2000 he changed his mind and signed an NBA contract in August of that year with the Vancouver Grizzlies. After the end of that season, he played for teams in Italy, Greece, Russia, and Japan.

Reflecting on his experience, in 2016, Abdul-Rauf recognized his sacrifice, but was proud of his principled stand. "I want to live and die with a free conscience and a free soul when it's all said and done. That's the journey I'm on," he stated. "I had to make that decision for myself and I found that after I did that, it took off a huge weight. Do you get ridiculed? Do you hear the nonsense? Do people try to assassinate your character? Yes, but when it's all said and done, you're like, man, I feel good because I know that I'm standing on something I believe in" (Washington 2016).

Further Reading

Hodges, Jim. 1996. "NBA Sits Abdul-Rauf for Stance on Anthem." *Los Angeles Times*, March 13, 1996. http://articles.latimes.com/1996-03-13/sports/sp -46409_1_mahmoud-abdul-rauf

Maisonet, Eddie. 2014. "Mahmoud Abdul-Rauf: Here, Gone and Quickly Forgotten." *SB Nation* (blog), March 25, 2014. https://www.sbnation.com/2014/ 3/25/5544920/mahmoud-abdul-rauf-nuggets-national-anthem

Seifert, Kevin. 2018. "How National Anthem Rules Differ across Sports Leagues." ESPN, May 24, 2018. http://www.espn.com/nfl/story/_/id/20848575/ rules-national-anthem-differ-sports-leagues

Washington, Jesse. 2016. "Still No Anthem, Still No Regrets for Mahmoud Abdul-Rauf." *The Undefeated*, September 1, 2016. https://theundefeated.com/ features/abdul-rauf-doesnt-regret-sitting-out-national-anthem/

The NFL Mandates Players Be on the Field for the National Anthem (2009)

Until 2009, the NFL did not require players, coaches, or other team personnel to be on the field during the national anthem. Instead, each individual had the option of staying in the locker room until game time. Over the years, a custom developed: NFL teams exited the locker rooms and were on the sidelines during the pregame activities for Sunday afternoon games. If teams were on the field, they were encouraged to stand for the national anthem out of respect for flag and country.

However, the custom for primetime games was different. These games were broadcast during primetime evening viewing hours on premier NFL programs like *Monday Night Football,* which received high ratings for many years. By the early years of the twenty-first century, primetime games were also shown on Thursday, Friday, Saturday, and Sunday nights. For these pre-2009 primetime games, players traditionally remained in the locker room until they were introduced to the TV audience. The emergence of players from the tunnel was part of the entertainment and took place after the anthem played.

On special occasions, such as the Super Bowl and tributes to active military and military veterans during wartime, teams stood together on the sidelines for the national anthem and other patriotic events during primetime games. However, there was no NFL rule requiring the practice.

The confusing language on when NFL players and coaches should be on the sidelines confused many fans, teams, and commentators. To address the problem, the NFL made a policy shift, saying players should present themselves on the sidelines before every game. As one NFL spokesperson observed, "We decided to make it consistent across all games, as it was the right thing to do" (Roberts 2017).

The NFL Game Operations Manual

The NFL did not craft its policy shift from scratch. Instead, it was based on language existing since 1978 in the NFL game operations manual.

The game operations manual contains more than 200 procedures and policies that dictate the conditions under which games are played. As described by the NFL, "The league's Game Operations Department uses the manual to govern the conduct of home clubs, to ensure that they protect players and provide the conditions for a fair and fan-friendly contest. Clubs face warnings and other penalties for noncompliance" (NFL.com 2018). The manual differs from the NFL Rulebook, which governs the rules of the game itself; for example, the rulebook dictates yardage penalties for player infractions like "illegal motion," "unsportsmanlike conduct," and "pass interference," as well as specific procedures for challenging an official's call.

The game operations manual is sent out to teams every year, but it is not available to the public. In 2009, the manual's policy regarding the national anthem, unchanged since 1978, read: "The National Anthem must be played prior to every NFL game, and all players must be on the sideline for the National Anthem. During the National Anthem, players on the field and bench area should stand at attention, face the flag, hold helmets in their left hand, and refrain from talking" (NFL.com 2018).

Individuals and teams that do not follow NFL policy face consequences. "It should be pointed out to players and coaches that we continue to be judged by the public in this area of respect for the flag and our country. Failure to be on the field by the start of the National Anthem may result in discipline, such as fines, suspensions, and/or the forfeiture of draft choice(s) for violations of the above, including first offenses" (Fitzpatrick 2017).

Continued Confusion over the National Anthem Policy

The NFL hoped its 2009 policy shift would clear up any confusion about where teams were *supposed to be* during pregame festivities, including the playing of the national anthem. However, it did not explain what the players, coaches, and team personnel were *required to do* during that time.

The confusion can be traced to the language used in the games operation manual. The policy dictated that players *must* be on the sidelines for the national anthem, but that they *should* stand respectfully for it. Therefore, players were not *required* to stand or put their hands over their hearts for the national anthem. This distinction did not cause any controversy or confusion until the 2016 season, when NFL players began protesting racial inequality and police brutality by kneeling on the sidelines during the national anthem.

The Paid Patriotism Controversy

In 2015, a report released by Republican senators from Arizona John McCain and Jeff Flake detailed the results of an investigation into payments made by the Department of Defense (DoD) to professional sports leagues, including the NFL, Major League Baseball (MLB), the National Basketball Association (NBA), and the National Hockey League (NHL). The investigation found evidence that the DoD paid millions of dollars to these leagues between 2012 and 2015 to hold events honoring the U.S. military, including "on-field color guard performances, enlistment and re-enlistment ceremonies, performances of the national anthem, full-field flag details, and ceremonial first pitch and puck drops" (Flake and McCain 2015). The report noted the DoD paid NFL teams $6 million, out of a total $9.1 million to all sports leagues (Theobald 2015).

Some fans and commentators believe the NFL's 2009 policy shift was made in response to the DoD practice of paying professional sports franchises to host patriotic performances, military events, and national anthem performances. In other words, perhaps the NFL made its policy shift in order to please the DoD. The matter became known as the Paid Patriotism controversy. In their defense, league officials pointed out the NFL implemented its policy shift three years before any DoD payments began. In addition, they pointed out the report gave no evidence of a connection between the 2009 policy shift and the payments.

In 2015, the NFL stopped accepting payments from the DoD. In fact, it paid back more than $720,000 of taxpayer money, the only major sports league to do so. The report concludes, "Americans deserve the ability to assume that tributes for our men and women in military uniform are genuine displays of patriotic pride, which many are, rather than taxpayer-funded DoD marketing gimmicks" (Flake and McCain 2015).

The Impact of the NFL Protests on the 2009 Policy

When NFL players began protesting institutional racism and police brutality during the national anthem in 2016, many fans and commentators assumed the NFL had a rule against players sitting on the bench or kneeling on the sidelines during the national anthem. There was even a viral meme on social media falsely claiming there was a rule to that effect in the NFL Rulebook.

In response, the NFL addressed the confusion. First, NFL spokesman Brian McCarthy explained there was a *policy* on the national anthem issue. "It's policy, not a rule," he stated. "I think where people are getting confused is, rules, that's like holding or defensive pass interference, that's a rule. This is policy" (Carter 2017). Second, the policy was contained in the game operations manual, not the NFL Rulebook. Furthermore, McCarthy clarified that players were not required to stand for the anthem. "Players are encouraged but not required to stand during the playing of the national anthem" (Willingham 2017).

Debate over the NFL protests led to increasing calls for the league to enact a stronger policy on the matter. President Donald Trump was one of the most vocal critics of the 2009 policy, arguing that players should be required to stand for the national anthem out of respect for the flag, the military, and the country. Throughout the 2017–2018 season, the NFL struggled to defend its policy in light of increasing public pressure and the perception of some NFL officials and team owners that the protest was the main reason for falling fan attendance at games and flat television ratings.

Further Reading

Carter, Allison. 2017. "What the NFL Policy Book Says about the National Anthem." *Indianapolis Star*, September 25, 2017. https://www.indystar.com/story/news/2017/09/25/what-nfl-rule-book-actually-says-national-anthem/699886001/

Fitzpatrick, Alex. 2017. "Does the NFL Require Players to Stand for the National Anthem?" *Time*, September 25, 2017. http://time.com/4955704/nfl-league-rulebook-a62-63-national-anthem-rule/

Flake, Jeff, and John McCain. 2015. *Tackling Paid Patriotism: A Joint Oversight Report*. https://www.mccain.senate.gov/public/_cache/files/12de6dcb-d8d8-4a58-8795-562297f948c1/tackling-paid-patriotism-oversight-report.pdf

National Football League. 2018. "League Governance." https://operations.nfl.com/football-ops/league-governance/

Roberts, Daniel. 2017. "There's No 'NFL Rule' That Players Must Stand for the Anthem—But There's a 'Policy'." *Yahoo*, September 25, 2017. https://finance.yahoo.com/news/theres-no-nfl-rule-players-must-stand-anthem-theres-policy-162020168.html

Willingham, A. J. 2017. "The National Anthem in Sports (Spoiler: It Wasn't Always This Way)." CNN, September 25, 2017. https://www.cnn.com/2017/09/25/us/nfl-national-anthem-trump-kaepernick-history-trnd/index.html

St. Louis Rams Protest Police Brutality (2014)

On August 9, 2014, Darren Wilson, a white police officer in Ferguson, Missouri, shot and killed Michael Brown, an 18-year-old African American. The fatal incident set off ignited protests from members of the community, which quickly dominated social media and attracted international attention. Over the next few months, people marched in the streets of Ferguson, a northern suburb of St. Louis. These demonstrations sometimes turned violent. The outcry over Brown's death also generated protests from five players on the St. Louis Rams, sparking a larger conversation over the role of social justice protests at sporting events.

An Incident in Ferguson

The chain of events that led to the death of Michael Brown began when the young man entered a local convenience store the morning of August 9, 2014. A security camera showed him shoving a clerk and taking a box of cigars. The incident was reported to police. Following up on the description of the suspect, police officer Darren Wilson spotted Brown walking down the street with a friend. Wilson pulled his squad car alongside him to question him. According to Wilson, Brown leaned in through the car window and tried to grab Wilson's gun. Brown subsequently fled, pursued by Wilson. When Brown stopped, turned, and allegedly charged at Wilson, the police officer shot him, hitting him six times.

Initial witness accounts stated Brown had turned around and put his hands up in surrender. There were also witness reports that he may have said "don't shoot" to Wilson right before his death. These accounts led many to believe Wilson had shot an unarmed man who was trying to surrender to authorities. A later Federal Bureau of Investigation (FBI) report, however, found no evidence that Brown raised his hands or said anything to Wilson.

The unrest in Ferguson began just a few days after Brown's death and stretched over a period of several months. Demonstrators used the rallying cry "hands up, don't shoot" and raised their hands in mock surrender to symbolize not only Brown's death but also the police shootings of other unarmed black men like Brown.

On August 14, President Barack Obama addressed the nation after several days of violence and rioting in the streets of Ferguson, asking for calm. Authorities were particularly concerned over escalating tensions between protesters and police officers; protesters criticized law enforcement's response to demonstrations, while police officers reported feeling targeted and unfairly judged by protesters.

After a grand jury decided on November 27 not to indict Wilson for Brown's shooting, demonstrators once again took to the streets. Many Americans believed Wilson had gotten away with shooting Brown in cold blood and made their frustration over the perceived injustice heard on the streets of Ferguson and on social media. Many other Americans, however, saw the decision as fair. It reflected their understanding of the situation— Wilson had a right to defend himself against a charging suspect who posed a deadly threat to his safety.

The St. Louis Rams "Hands Up, Don't Shoot" Protest

On November 30, 2014, the St. Louis Rams played the Oakland Raiders at the Edward Jones Dome in St. Louis, Missouri. As the Rams players exited the tunnel and ran onto the field, Stedman Bailey, Tavon Austin, Jared Cook, Chris Givens, and Kenny Britt stopped and gave the crowd a "hands up, don't shoot" gesture from the Ferguson demonstrations.

After the game, Britt, a Rams wide receiver, explained why he protested. "I don't want the people in the community to feel like we turned a blind eye to it," he stated. "What would I like to see happen? Change in America" (Howard 2014).

Rams tight end Cook regarded his actions as a show of solidarity with Ferguson demonstrators. "We kind of came collectively together and decided we wanted to do something," he recalled. "We haven't been able to go down to Ferguson to do anything because we have been busy. Secondly, it's kind of dangerous down there and none of us want to get caught up in anything. So we wanted to come out and show our respect to the protests and the people who have been doing a heck of a job around the world" (Wagoner 2014).

A few days later, Cook also clarified his respect for law enforcement. "Why would we come at the police in a disrespectful way when we work with the police in the community all the time?" he asked. "The police are up here every day. There were four police cars here this morning when I pulled into work. The police have picnics during the summer in our parking lot where they bring their kids and children to meet and greet and have fun with us. So why would I disrespect a group of men that we have complete respect for in the community that helps us every day?" (Martin 2014).

He argued the protest should be regarded as an example of how to demonstrate peacefully. "'Hands up, don't shoot' is not just a Ferguson thing," he asserted. "It's a worldwide thing. People are doing it in New York. People are doing it in Florida. People are doing it on the West Coast. It's not just about Ferguson. It's a message worldwide that for young adults that you can protest and you can do things peacefully without getting out of line" (Martin 2014).

Reaction to the Player Protest

One of the strongest reactions to the player protest was from the St. Louis Police Officers Association (SLPOA). After the game, the group released a statement. They called for the five Rams players who protested to be disciplined. They also demanded a public apology from the NFL.

"I know that there are those that will say that these players are simply exercising their First Amendment rights," SLPOA business manager Jeff Roorda maintained. "Well, I've got news for people who think that way: Cops have first amendment rights too, and we plan to exercise ours. I'd remind the NFL and their players that it is not the violent thugs burning down buildings that buy their advertiser's products. It's cops and the good people of St. Louis and other NFL towns that do. Somebody needs to throw a flag on this play. If it's not the NFL and the Rams, then it'll be cops and their supporters" (Wagoner 2014).

NFL spokesman Brian McCarthy responded: "We respect and understand the concerns of all individuals who have expressed views on this tragic situation" (Wagoner 2014).

At a press conference the day after the game, then Rams coach Jeff Fisher announced that the five players who participated in the protests would not be fined. "As far as the choice that the players made, no, they were exercising their right to free speech," he said. "They will not be disciplined by the club nor will they be disciplined by the National Football League as it was released today" (ESPN, 2014).

A few days later, officials from the SLPOA met with team officials to share their views and find a way a way forward. Roorda reported that talks were fruitful and would continue.

Coach Fisher also expressed his intentions to move forward after the protest. "It's my personal opinion, and I firmly believe, that it's important that I keep sports and politics separate," he said. "I'm a head coach. I'm not a politician, an activist, or an expert on societal issues. So I'm going to answer questions about the game" (Thomas 2014).

Further Reading

Associated Press. 2014. "Rams Raise Arms in Show of Solidarity." *USA Today*, November 30, 2014. https://www.usatoday.com/story/sports/nfl/2014/11/ 30/rams-raise-arms-in-show-of-solidarity/19716529/

ESPN. 2014. "No Fines for Rams Players' Salute." ESPN, December 2, 2014. http:// www.espn.com/nfl/story/_/id/11963218/the-five-st-louis-rams-players-saluted -slain-teenager-michael-brown-sunday-game-not-fined

Howard, Adam. 2014. "St. Louis Rams Players Show Solidarity with Ferguson Protesters." MSNBC, December 1, 2014. http://www.msnbc.com/msnbc/ st-louis-rams-show-solidarity-ferguson-protesters

Martin, Jill. 2014. "Rams Player Says He Received Threats after 'Hands Up, Don't Shoot' Protest." CNN, December 4, 2014. https://www.cnn.com/2014/12/ 04/us/rams-threats-ferguson/index.html

Thomas, Jim. 2014. "Police Group Wants Rams Players Disciplined for 'Hands Up' Gesture; NFL Declines." *St. Louis Post-Dispatch*, December 1, 2014. https:// www.stltoday.com/sports/football/professional/police-group-wants-rams -players-disciplined-for-hands-up-gesture/article_aac1b733-ad65-5b54 -a60b-7c616baef983.html

Wagoner, Nick. 2014. "Rams Players Salute Ferguson." ESPN, December 1, 2014. http://www.espn.com/nfl/story/_/id/11958985/st-louis-rams-give-pregame -salute-ferguson-missouri

University of Missouri Protests Force President's Resignation (2015)

On February 26, 2010, two white students at the University of Missouri were caught scattering cotton balls on the grounds in front of the Gaines/ Oldham Black Cultural Center on campus. While the students, Sean Fitzgerald and Zachary Taylor, claimed the act was a harmless prank, many students saw racist connotations to placing cotton on the property of a black student center, as if a threatening reminder of slavery. As Deputy Chancellor Michael Middleton observed, "This incident was much more, in our view, than a childish prank" (Sunne 2010). The students were sentenced to community service.

A similar incident on campus occurred a year later, when a white student was caught spray painting a racist slur on a statue outside of a campus building. The student, Benjamin Elliot, pleaded guilty to misdemeanor property damage and was sentenced to community service.

"One Mizzou"

These racist acts on the University of Missouri campus led to a diversity campaign called "One Mizzou." It fostered a culture of respect and responsibility among the different communities at the university. Mizzou is a long-standing nickname for the University of Missouri.

Initially, administrators and students were optimistic about the campaign. Soon after the "One Mizzou" campaign launched, however, other departments starting using the slogan for advertising and fundraising. Within a few years, the slogan seemed to be ubiquitous on campus, which many students believe diluted its message.

Shooting in Ferguson

The shooting of Michael Brown, a young, unarmed black man, by white police officer Darren Wilson on August 9, 2014, provoked racial tensions on the University of Missouri campus. Brown's shooting occurred in Ferguson, a northern suburb of St. Louis approximately 120 miles from Columbia, the site of the university's main campus.

As people marched in response to Brown's death in Ferguson and participated in online campaigns like Black Lives Matter, conversations about the systematic oppression of and violence against African Americans at the hands of law enforcement took place at numerous universities, including the University of Missouri. Students and instructors from the university demonstrated in Ferguson and Columbia against police brutality and other incidents of racial discrimination.

For many students, however, the university wasn't doing enough to address the simmering racial tensions on campus. Jonathan Butler, a graduate student and social justice activist, observed that the university missed an opportunity and in the process showed that there were "racially motivated things—murders, assaults, other things—that happen and we are just going to sweep them under the rug" (Miller 2015).

Social Media Post Sparks Debate

On September 12, 2015, a Facebook post by University of Missouri student government president Payton Head brought the issue of racial, transgender, and anti-gay discrimination on campus to the forefront for Mizzou students and officials. In his post, which subsequently went viral, Head described an incident in which two people riding in the back of a truck screamed racist slurs at him while he was walking across campus.

"I really just want to know why my simple existence is such a threat to society," he asked. "For those of you who wonder why I'm always talking about the importance of inclusion and respect, it's because I've experienced moments like this multiple times at THIS university, making me feel not included here" (People's Power Assemblies 2015).

A few days later, R. Bowen Loftin, the university's chancellor, responded in a statement. "We will be continuing our efforts to respond to the concerns that have been raised and to employ working groups relative to the steps we must take as a university and a community to live up to our values. Please help us make this campus a safe and productive learning and living environment and show our community and the world that Mizzou will not tolerate hate" (Loftin 2015).

Many students saw the university's response as lackluster and ineffective. Students held two "Racism Lives Here" rallies on campus to pressure the administration to more effectively address the issues brought up in Head's Facebook post.

Student concerns were validated just a few weeks later when a drunk white student walked on a stage and disrupted about 15 members of the Legion of Black Collegians, the university's black student government, during a rehearsal of the group's role in homecoming festivities. When asked to leave, the student used a racist slur.

In response, Warren Michael Davis, the head of the Legion of Black Collegians, released a statement that challenged the administration to be proactive and take the issue seriously. "To the administrators who have been so kind as to organize countless panels and committees to address the issue of diversity on this wasteland of a campus, please just stop," the statement read. "At this point it is evident to me that you are attempting to create a diversion (like you always do), that will appease the underrepresented population on this campus until our leadership either graduates or tires of the fight" (@MizzouLBC October 5, 2015).

A few days later, Chancellor Loftin agreed in a statement that the university had not done enough to address racism on campus and proposed a number of steps, including diversity and inclusion training for all students and faculty. Students and activists considered Loftin's proposal a good first step, but ultimately not enough to effectively address racism on campus.

A Pivotal Incident

On October 10, 2015, during the University of Missouri homecoming parade, a group of protesters blocked the convertible driven by university president Tim Wolfe. The parade came to a halt, and bystanders shouted the protesters down. Police began to remove protesters from the parade route. Wolfe moved his car forward, tapping Butler, who was one of the demonstrators. Butler was unharmed, but the incident led to charges that Wolfe was aggressive and insensitive to the protestors and that police used excessive force in removing them from the parade route. In the early aftermath of the incident, Wolfe did not issue an apology, further inflaming racial tension on campus.

Concerned Student 1950, a student group named for the year African American students were first admitted to the University of Missouri, issued a list of demands on October 20. The eight demands included a handwritten apology from Wolfe, his removal as president of the university system, an increase in the numbers of black faculty and staff, funding to create programs to help minority students and enrich diversity on campus, and other programs to facilitate an accepting environment.

A few days later, Wolfe met with members of Concerned Student 1950 to discuss their demands. When it was reported that Wolfe did not agree to the demands, Butler launched a hunger strike on November 3, saying it would continue until Wolfe resigned. "I already feel like campus is an unlivable space," he explained. "So it's worth sacrificing something of this grave amount, because I'm already not wanted here. I'm already treated like I'm not a human" (Miller 2015). The next day, students announced a boycott in support of Butler. Many staff and faculty members walked off the job.

On November 6, Wolfe issued an apology to Concerned Student 1950 for his reaction to the homecoming demonstration. He also acknowledged the pervasive racism on campus. "I am sorry this is the case," he stated. "I truly want all members of our university community to feel included, valued, and safe" (Mallory 2015). He also expressed concern for Butler's health, then five days into a hunger strike.

The Mizzou Football Team Takes a Position

In support of the student boycott, several African American players on the university's football team announced they would not practice or play until Wolfe was removed. The athletes of color on the University of Missouri football team truly believe "Injustice Anywhere Is a Threat to Justice Everywhere," the group's statement read. "We will no longer participate in any football-related activities until President Tim Wolfe resigns or is removed due to his negligence toward marginalized students' experiences. WE ARE UNITED!!!" (@MizzouLBC October 5, 2015).

Within hours, the rest of the team joined the boycott. The team's coaching staff and the university's athletic department stood in solidarity with the team as well. The football team's boycott attracted nationwide attention to the issue of racism on the Mizzou campus. Reports estimated that if the football protests continued, the team's upcoming game with Brigham Young University would have to be cancelled, costing the University of Missouri more than $1 million in revenue.

On November 9, 2015, Wolfe resigned. "I ask everybody—from students to faculty to staff to my friends, everybody—use my resignation to heal and to start talking again," he urged. "To make the changes necessary, and let's focus on what we can change today and in the future, and not what we can't change, which is what happened in the past" (Wolfe 2015).

Further Reading

Hibsch, Jimmy. 2011. "'One Mizzou' Diversity Campaign Unveiled." *The Maneater*, April 8, 2011. https://www.themaneater.com/stories/campus/one-mizzou -diversity-campaign-unveiled

Legion of Black Collegians (@MizzouLBC). 2015a. Twitter, October 5, 2015. https://twitter.com/MizzouLBC/status/651111018576277504

Legion of Black Collegians (@MizzouLBC). 2015b. Twitter, November 7, 2015. https://twitter.com/MizzouLBC/status/663177684428566532

Loftin, Bowen. 2015. Facebook, September 17, 2015. https://www.facebook.com/ Mizzou/posts/from-chancellor-r-bowen-loftin/10153016957861512/

Malloy, Quinn. 2015. "Wolfe Issues Apology to Concerned Student 1950." *The Maneater*, November 6, 2015. https://www.themaneater.com/stories/ uwire/wolfe-issues-apology-concerned-student-1950

Miller, Michael E. 2015. "Black Grad Student on Hunger Strike in Mo. after Swastika Drawn with Human Feces." *Washington Post*, November 6, 2015. https://www.washingtonpost.com/news/morning-mix/wp/2015/11/06/ black-grad-student-on-hunger-strike-in-mo-after-swastika-drawn-with -human-feces/?utm_term=.b27039409cc8

People's Power Assemblies. 2015. Facebook, September 12, 2015. https:// www.facebook.com/PeoplesPowerAssemblies/posts/932921543409524

Sunne, Samantha. 2010. "Students Sentenced for Cotton Ball Incident." *The Maneater*, April 29, 2010. https://www.themaneater.com/stories/campus/ students-sentenced-cotton-ball-incident

Wolfe, Tim. 2015. "Transcript of Resignation Speech." *Missourian*, November 9, 2015. https://www.columbiamissourian.com/news/higher_education/ transcript-of-wolfe-s-resignation-speech/article_b666ff76-8703-11e5 -896f-87b19edd2aed.html

Wynn, Sarah. 2015. "Administrators Discontinue One Mizzou, Developing New Marketing Campaign This Summer." *The Maneater*, June 3, 2015. https:// www.themaneater.com/stories/uwire/administrators-developing-new -marketing-campaign-s

Colin Kaepernick Refuses to Stand for the National Anthem (2016)

On August 14, 2016, San Francisco 49ers quarterback Colin Kaepernick declined to stand for the national anthem at the team's home game against the Houston Texans, choosing to sit on the bench by himself. At the time, his actions did not get much attention, possibly because Kaepernick was out of uniform, recovering from shoulder surgery as well as knee and thumb injuries. Kaepernick did not speak to the press after the game.

Kaepernick again sat on the bench in his street clothes during the national anthem at the next preseason game on August 20 against the Denver Broncos. Once again, his protest went unmentioned in press coverage of the game.

On August 26, 2016, the 49ers played the Green Bay Packers in the preseason's third game. This time, Kaepernick was scheduled to play and wore his uniform. During the anthem, Jennifer Lee Chan, a beat writer for *NinersNation.com*, took a picture of the team on the sidelines. Chan's photograph clearly showed Kaepernick sitting on the bench alone as the rest of his teammates stood in a row for the anthem. When she tweeted the image after the game, the press finally took notice.

The Origins of Kaepernick's Protest

When interviewed about the August 26 game, Kaepernick explained that he sat in protest of what he described as systematic racism in the United States. "I am not going to stand up to show pride in a flag for a country that oppresses black people and people of color," Kaepernick explained. "To me, this is bigger than football and it would be selfish on my part to look the other way. There are bodies on the street and people getting paid leave and getting away with murder" (Wyche 2016).

Kaepernick referred to a series of incidents during the previous few years in which police or private citizens killed unarmed African American men and teenagers. A new civil rights organization called Black Lives Matter emerged to confront incidents of police mistreatment of African Americans and other groups. After high-profile incidents of police brutality against people of color, Black Lives Matter and other activist groups organized demonstrations that captured media attention and inspired more athletes and celebrities to take part in marches, online campaigns, and community activism.

Only a month before Kaepernick's protests began, two police officers shot and killed a young black man, Alton Sterling, at close range while he lay on the ground in Baton Rouge, Louisiana, on June 5, 2016. Later, the officers said they shot Sterling because they thought he was reaching for a gun allegedly tucked in the waistband of his pants. Bystanders filmed the confrontation, and the video sparked widespread outrage and calls for justice. Kaepernick expressed his anger on Instagram. "This is what lynchings look like in 2016!" he posted. "Another murder in the streets because the color of a man's skin, at the hands of people who say they will protect us" (@kaepernick7 July 7, 2016).

Sterling's death deeply affected Kaepernick's teammate, Eric Reid. He approached Kaepernick to discuss how the two of them could bring awareness to the issues that mattered to them. "We spoke at length about many of the issues that face our community, including systematic oppression of people of color, police brutality, and the criminal justice system," recalled Reid. "We also discussed how we could use our platform, provided to us by being professional athletes in the N.F.L., to speak for those who are voiceless" (Reid 2017).

Even though Kaepernick was supported by Reid and other players throughout the league, his actions and statements also brought scorching criticism from league officials, politicians, sports commentators, and fans. Many supported his right to protest but saw his decision to sit during the national anthem as unpatriotic and inappropriate.

One such critic was Nate Boyer, a former NFL player and Green Beret, who wrote Kaepernick an open letter published in the August 30, 2016, edition of the *Army Times*. Boyer's letter suggested Kaepernick's action implied disrespect for the sacrifices of active soldiers and military veterans. However, he closed with a vow to be respectful of other opinions. "There are already plenty [of] people fighting fire with fire, and it's just not helping anyone or anything. So I'm just going to keep listening, with an open mind" (Boyer 2016).

Boyer's letter prompted a meeting between him, Kaepernick, and Reid to find a more respectful way for players to protest racism and police brutality. During the meeting, Boyer suggested kneeling during the anthem. Kneeling, he explained, was a symbolic way soldiers honored fallen comrades. It was considered a solemn and powerful gesture.

Taking a Knee

On September 1, 2016, before a game between the 49ers and the San Diego Chargers, both Kaepernick and Reid took a knee, an action involving kneeling on one knee, for the first time during the playing of the national anthem. Boyer, who was invited on the sidelines, stood alongside the two men with his hand over his heart. A number of league players joined the protests in following weeks.

Later, after receiving Amnesty International's Ambassador of Conscience Award in 2018, Kaepernick discussed his decision to kneel during the national anthem. "How can you stand for the national anthem of a nation that preaches and propagates, 'freedom and justice for all,' that is so unjust to so many of the people living there?" he asked. "How can you not be in a rage when you know that you are always at risk of death in the streets or enslavement in the prison system? How can you be willingly blind to the truth of systematic racialized injustice? When Malcolm X said, 'I'm for the truth no matter who tells it. I'm for justice no matter who it is for or against. I'm a human being, first and foremost, and as such I'm for whoever and whatever benefits humanity as a whole.' I took that to heart" (Kaepernick 2018).

Further Reading

Boyer, Nate. 2016. "An Open Letter to Colin Kaepernick, from a Green Beret-Turned-Long Snapper." *Army Times*, August 30, 2016. https://www.armytimes.com/opinion/2016/08/30/an-open-letter-to-colin-kaepernick-from-a-green-beret-turned-long-snapper/

Kaepernick, Colin (@kaepernick7). 2016. Instagram video, July 6, 2016. https://www.instagram.com/p/BHhetl8g_EE/

Kaepernick, Colin. 2018. "Amnesty International's Ambassador of Conscience Award: Transcript of Speech." *Amnesty International*, April 21, 2018. https://www.amnesty.nl/content/uploads/2018/04/Colin-Kaepernicks-Speech-Ambassador-of-Conscience-Final.pdf?x66178

Reid, Eric. 2017. "Why Colin Kaepernick and I Decided to Take a Knee." *New York Times*, September 23, 2017. https://www.nytimes.com/2017/09/25/opinion/colin-kaepernick-football-protests.html

Wyche, Steve. 2016. "Colin Kaepernick Explains Why He Sat during National Anthem." NFL, August 28, 2016. http://www.nfl.com/news/story/0ap3000000691077/article/colin-kaepernick-explains-protest-of-national-anthem

Trump Calls for the Firing of Protesting NFL Players (2017)

By the start of the 2017–2018 season, the NFL protests were a hot-button topic on sports talk radio and political shows on cable TV networks. About a month into the regular season, President Donald Trump jumped into the debate with his strongest criticism of the protests to that point. On September 22, 2017, he ripped into the protesters during a rally in Alabama, criticizing the players as unpatriotic and disrespectful. Moreover, he urged NFL owners to fire any player participating in the protests. "Wouldn't you love to see one of these NFL owners, when somebody disrespects our flag, to say 'Get that son of a b**** off that field right now! Out! He's fired. He's fired!'" (Graham 2017).

Trump complained football was being ruined by overzealous officiating and concern over injuries. He railed against what he saw as the disrespect shown by players during the national anthem. "But you know what's hurting the game more than [too much officiating to protect players from injuries]? When people like yourself turn on television and you see those people taking the knee when they are playing our great national anthem. The only thing you could do better is if you see it, even if it's one player, leave the stadium. I guarantee things will stop. Things will stop. Just pick up and leave. Pick up and leave. Not the same game anymore, anyway" (Jenkins 2017).

Trump and the NFL Protests

The president's September 2017 criticisms were not his first on the issue. In fact, Trump had slammed the protests from the start. On August 29, 2016, then candidate Trump called out Colin Kaepernick by name during a radio interview. "I have followed [the protests] and I think personally it's not a good thing," he stated. "I think it's a terrible thing, and you know, maybe he should find a country that works better for him, let him try, it's not going to happen" (NFL 2016).

A few months later, Trump once again focused on Kaepernick's role in the protests during a rally in Colorado. This time, however, he cited Kaepernick and the excitement over the presidential race for the NFL's falling television ratings. "I don't know if you know," he told the crowd, "but the NFL is way down in their ratings. And you know why? Two reasons. Number one is, this politics they're finding is a rougher game than football, and more exciting. Honestly, we've taken a lot of people away from the NFL. And the other reason is Kaepernick. Kaepernick" (*Sports Illustrated* 2016). On November 8, 2016, Trump was elected president. Despite his new role, he continued his attacks on Kaepernick and the NFL.

On March 3, 2017, Kaepernick became a free agent. A few weeks later, a report surfaced that he remained unsigned because there were some teams who feared the team that signed Kaepernick would be bombarded with critical tweets and comments, not only from disapproving fans but also from Trump (Freeman 2017).

A few days after that report surfaced, Trump bragged about his influence on NFL owners at a rally in Louisville, Kentucky. "But there was an article today, it was reported by NFL owners don't want to pick [Kaepernick] up because they don't want to get a nasty tweet from Donald Trump. Do you believe that? I just saw that. I just saw that. I said if I remember that one I'm going to report it to the people of Kentucky. Because they like it when people actually stand for the American flag" (Florio 2017).

Kaepernick was not signed by an NFL team during the 2017 season. Other players chose to protest in the first few games, but it was widely believed that the protests would wind down as the season continued and that the players would find another way to raise awareness about their social justice concerns. Trump's insults at the Alabama rally in September, however, led the entire NFL to rebuke him and unify behind the idea of free speech. It also renewed accusations that Trump's focus on Kaepernick and other NFL protesters—most of whom were African American—was meant to divide the country along racial lines.

Support for Trump's Position

In light of criticism that his rhetoric was deliberately divisive, President Trump denied that his words were racist or designed to inflame racial tensions for political purposes. "This has nothing to do with race," he argued. "I never said anything about race. This has nothing to do with race or anything else. This has to do with respect for our country and respect for our flag" (Tynes 2017).

According to a number of polls, a majority approved of the president's views. A CBS News poll found that 52 percent of Americans disapproved of the NFL protests during the anthem, while 38 percent approved. The poll also showed that 48 percent disapproved of Trump's criticisms of the protests, while 38 percent approved (De Pinto et al. 2017). Trump's Republican base voters were especially supportive.

Trump continued to condemn the NFL protests at subsequent rallies and on social media, still arguing that the player protests were disrespectful to military, flag, and country. The media blamed the persistent controversy for flat attendance and declining TV ratings during the 2017–2018 NFL season.

Further Reading

De Pinto, Jennifer, Fred Backus, Kabir Khanna, and Anthony Salvanto. 2017. "Democrats, Republicans Divide over NFL Protests, Trump Comments-Poll." *CBS News*, September 29, 2017. https://www.cbsnews.com/news/democrats-republicans-divide-over-nfl-players-protests-trump-comments-poll/

Florio, Mike. 2017. "Donald Trump Calls Out Colin Kaepernick, Again." *NBC Sports*, March 20, 2017. https://profootballtalk.nbcsports.com/2017/03/20/donald-trump-calls-out-colin-kaepernick-again/

Freeman, Mike. 2017. "Colin Kaepernick Sentenced to NFL Limbo for the Crime of Speaking His Mind." *Bleacher Report*, March 17, 2017. https://bleacherreport.com/articles/2698098-colin-kaepernick-sentenced-to-nfl-limbo-for-the-crime-of-speaking-his-mind

Graham, Bryan Armen. 2017. "Donald Trump Blasts NFL Anthem Protesters: 'Get That Son of a B**** off the Field'." *The Guardian*, September 23, 2017. https://www.theguardian.com/sport/2017/sep/22/donald-trump-nfl-national-anthem-protests

Jenkins, Aric. 2017. "Read President Trump's NFL Speech on National Anthem Protests." *Time*, September 23, 2017. http://time.com/4954684/donald-trump-nfl-speech-anthem-protests/

King, Peter. 2017. "Monday Morning QB: Response to President Trump Made Roger Goodell 'Proud of Our League'." *Sports Illustrated*, September 25, 2017. https://www.si.com/nfl/2017/09/25/nfl-anthem-protests-roger-goodell-president-trump-week-3-peter-king

National Football League. 2016. "Donald Trump on Kaepernick: Find Another Country." NFL.com, August 29, 2016. http://www.nfl.com/news/story/0ap3000000692256/article/donald-trump-on-kaepernick-find-another-country

Sports Illustrated. 2016. "Trump: NFL's Ratings Are Down because of Colin Kaepernick." *Sports Illustrated,* October 30, 2016. https://www.si.com/nfl/2016/10/30/donald-trump-nfl-ratings-down-colin-kaepernick

Tynes, Tyler. 2017. "Donald Trump Says His Comments on NFL Player Protest 'Have Nothing to Do with Race'." *SB Nation* (blog), September 24, 2017. https://www.sbnation.com/2017/9/24/16358682/donald-trump-says-nfl-protest-anthem-race

NFL Protests Spread in Response to Trump Criticisms (2017)

At a Huntsville, Alabama, political rally on September 22, 2017, President Donald Trump ripped into NFL players who protested during the national anthem. In front of a large group of supporters, he attacked them as unpatriotic and disrespectful and urged NFL owners to fire any player participating in the protests.

The next day, he repeated his condemnation on Twitter. "If a player wants the privilege of making millions of dollars in the NFL, or other leagues, he or she should not be allowed to disrespect our Great American Flag (or Country) and should stand for the National Anthem. If not, YOU'RE FIRED! Find something else to do!" (@realDonaldTrump September 23, 2017).

The NFL Reacts

NFL owners, league officials, team personnel, and players united against the president's attack. The NFL and team owners released statements saying Trump's comments were divisive while emphasizing the need for mutual respect and team unity. Owners and league officials expressed support for the activism and community involvement exhibited by NFL players. Many statements underscored the right to protest as a core American value and praised the courage of protesting players.

Many NFL players reacted to Trump's remarks with outrage. They asserted he was misinterpreting their protests, and they said his aggressive comments were a direct attack on their constitutional rights to free speech. Many players used the following week's games to show they would not be silenced or intimidated by the president. In many cases, team owners and personnel took part in these protests to show team unity.

On the Field

The first NFL game scheduled after the president's controversial remarks was the September 24 contest between the Jacksonville Jaguars and the Baltimore Ravens, which was played in Wembley Stadium in London, England (and therefore was broadcast early in the morning in the United States). During the national anthem, 27 players from both teams took a knee in protests—the most ever at a single NFL game. Players choosing not to take a knee instead locked arms in solidarity behind protesting players.

According to Ravens linebacker Terrell Suggs, the president's comments made it essential to take a side. "Personally, I think the comments made about my brothers who decided to protest and kneel is kind of what made us no longer be silent. We stand with our brothers. They have the right to protest. We knelt with them today. Nonviolent protest is as American as it gets. We knelt with them today and let them know that we are a unified front" (Hensley 2017).

After kickoff, Baltimore Ravens owner Steve Bisciotti released a statement on Twitter. "We recognize our players' influence. We respect their demonstration and support them 100 percent. All voices need to be heard. That's democracy in its highest form" (@Ravens September 24, 2017).

Several other teams staged similar pregame protests, taking a knee or raising a fist. A few sat on the sidelines. Many others decided not to take a knee and instead stood supportively behind kneeling players. Some who stood rested a hand on the shoulder of the kneeling player in front of them.

The Dallas Cowboys locked arms and took a knee before the anthem began, then stood together during it.

As they warmed up before the game, many Miami Dolphins players wore #IAMWITHKAP t-shirts to signal their solidarity with Colin Kaepernick. During the national anthem, a handful of Dolphins players took a knee while the rest of the team, coaches, and team owner Stephen Ross linked arms. On the opponent's sideline, every member of the New York Jets, including team owner Christopher Johnson, linked arms as well.

A few NFL teams chose to stay in the locker room during the anthem. The Seattle Seahawks released a statement explaining their team's decision. "As a team, we have decided that we will not participate in the national anthem. We will not stand for the injustice that has plagued people of color in this country. Out of love for our country and in honor of the sacrifices made on our behalf, we unite to oppose those that would deny our most basic freedoms. We remain committed in continuing to work towards equality and justice for all" (@seahawksPR September 24, 2017).

The Pittsburgh Steelers remained in the tunnel during the anthem because team members could not agree on how to respond to the president's attacks. Their attempt to avoid the controversy, however, was complicated when Steelers left tackle Alejandro Villaneuva, a military veteran, moved to the front of the tunnel to salute the flag during the anthem. Fans assumed that he had left his team behind and abandoned the protest, but Villaneuva later insisted that the team was behind him in the tunnel and he never intended to give the impression he had left his teammates behind.

In the weeks following the initial show of unity in the wake of Trump's September 23 remarks, NFL player protests continued on a smaller scale. The level of protest varied from team to team, however. Some teams, including the Philadelphia Eagles, Dallas Cowboys, and Chicago Bears, had no players taking a knee or sitting during the national anthem all season.

Vice President Mike Pence Joins the Fray

On October 8, 2017, Vice President Mike Pence and his wife Karen attended a game between the Indianapolis Colts and the San Francisco 49ers. After several 49er players took a knee during the anthem, Pence and his wife walked out.

Later that day, he tweeted a statement: "I left today's Colts game because President Trump and I will not dignify any event that disrespects our soldiers, our Flag, or our National Anthem. At a time when so many Americans are inspiring the nation with their courage, resolve, and resilience, now, more than ever, we should rally around our Flag and everything that unites us. While everyone is entitled to their own opinions, I don't think it's too much to ask NFL players to respect the Flag and our National Anthem. I stand with President Trump, I stand with our soldiers, and I will always stand with our Flag and our National Anthem" (@VP October 8, 2017).

Pence's tweet was supported by many fans and public officials. To them, the protests were unpatriotic. Some supported the player's right to protest but took issue with the forum or the timing.

However, others viewed Pence's walking out on the game as a public relations stunt. When Trump tweeted that he had asked Pence to walk out if protests on the field occurred, it confirmed the belief of some football fans that the whole event had been planned to generate more controversy and appeal to Trump's political base.

The NFL Considers a Policy Change

As the protests continued through the 2017 season, the NFL became concerned over the decline in TV ratings and game attendance. Although some attributed this to fewer people watching television overall and too many football games on television, others blamed it on the controversy over the NFL protests. Many league officials thought the controversy was driving away fans and advertisers.

On October 17, 2017, the NFL and the National Football League Players Association (NFLPA) met to discuss a possible change in policy regarding the national anthem. The two groups discussed the reasons behind the player protests and how the league, owners, players, and coaches and other personnel could come together to address those issues effectively. In a statement, the two groups said the meeting was productive.

Team owners were split on whether to enact a stronger policy that required players to stand during the anthem. Critics of the protests cited the decline in TV ratings and game attendance, viewing the controversy as a threat their business interests and too polarizing an issue for the sport. In a particularly divisive comment, Houston Texans owner Bob McNair asserted, "We can't have the inmates running the prison" (Wickersham and Van Natta Jr., 2017). McNair's comparison of African American players to prison inmates was considered racially insensitive and drew sharp criticism.

Several other team owners, however, felt that taking a hard line with players would only cause more friction. They felt it should be a priority to support players and work on the issues important to them. They expressed a hope that the problem would resolve over time.

NFL owners did not come up with a change on the national anthem policy. The issue was tabled until the next meetings in May 2018, which produced a change in policy that generated a firestorm of controversy from players and fans.

Further Reading

Baltimore Ravens (@Ravens). 2017. Twitter, September 24, 2017. https://twitter.com/Ravens/status/911952742301749248

Hensley, Jamison. 2017. "Ravens Linebacker Terrell Suggs on Why He Knelt during the Anthem." ESPN, September 24, 2017. http://www.espn.com/espn/now?nowId=21-40002869-4

Pence, Mike (@VP). 2017. Twitter, October 8, 2017. https://twitter.com/VP/status/917078269077413888

Seattle Seahawks (@seahawksPR). 2017. Twitter, September 24, 2017. https://twitter.com/seahawksPR/status/912038744408166401/

Stites, Adam. 2017. "NFL Players Responded to Donald Trump with More Protests Than Ever." *SB Nation* (blog), September 26, 2017. https://www.sbnation.com/2017/9/24/16354916/nfl-protest-national-anthem-donald-trump

Trump, Donald (@realDonaldTrump). 2017. Twitter, September 23, 2017. https://twitter.com/realDonaldTrump/status/911654284918880260

Wickersham, Seth, and Don Van Natta Jr. 2017. "Gaffes, TV Ratings Concerns Dominated as NFL, Players Forged Anthem Peace." *ESPN The Magazine*, October 27, 2017. http://www.espn.com/espn/otl/story/_/id/21170410/gaffes-tv-ratings-concerns-dominated-nfl-players-forged-anthem-peace-league-meetings

The NFL Creates a Controversial New Anthem Policy (2018)

Throughout the 2017–2018 season, NFL officials tried to find a compromise with the players on the issue of NFL player protests that respected their right to voice their concerns over social justice issues while at the same time addressing the perception that protesting during the national anthem was unpatriotic and disrespectful. Roger Goodell, the NFL commissioner, asserted that many fans misinterpreted the protests, seeing the players' actions as unpatriotic. "Players repeat over and over again this isn't about disrespect for our flag or military or our veterans. And I believe them," he stated. "But they also have to understand that it is interpreted much differently on a national basis" (Gleeson 2017).

Owners became increasingly concerned that the controversy over player protests during the national anthem resulted in flat TV ratings and attendance at games, which affected the teams' bottom lines. Finding a solution to the issue was essential to the financial well-being of the NFL.

A New Policy

On May 23, 2018, NFL owners announced a new national anthem policy at the conclusion of their spring meetings. Players and team personnel were required to stand if they were on the field during the anthem; however, players and team personnel had the option to stay in the locker room. Any violation of the agreement could result in a fine.

"The policy adopted today was approved in concert with the NFL's ongoing commitment to local communities and our country—one that is extraordinary in scope, resources, and alignment with our players," Goodell stated. "We are dedicated to continuing our collaboration with players to advance the goals of justice and fairness in all corners of our society" (Goodell 2018).

Support for the Policy

President Donald Trump supported the new anthem protest policy. "I think that's good," he remarked. "I don't think people should be staying in locker rooms but I still think it's good, you have to stand proudly for the national anthem. Or you shouldn't be playing, you shouldn't be there. Maybe you shouldn't be in the country. You have to stand proudly for the national anthem and the NFL owners did the right thing if that's what they've done" (NFL.com 2018).

NFL owners defended their new policy. On Twitter, Jacksonville Jaguars owner Shad Khan contended that it would not impact the players' fight for social justice. "We all want the same thing—respect for our nation and the flag, the focus on our game and a pledge to advancing social justice that will be absolute and stand the test of time. I believe that we're closer to that today, and I know that the Jacksonville Jaguars will be committed to those ideals this season and into the future" (@Jaguars, May 23, 2018).

Christopher Johnson, owner of the New York Jets, voted for the policy but announced his team would pay the fines for any Jets player fined for exercising freedom of speech. "I never want to put restrictions on the speech of our players," he explained. "Do I prefer that they stand? Of course. But I understand if they feel the need to protest. There are some big, complicated issues that we're all struggling with, and our players are on the front lines. I don't want to come down on them like a ton of bricks, and I won't. There will be no club fines or suspensions or any sort of repercussions. If the team gets fined, that's just something I'll have to bear" (Glauber 2018).

A number of NFL coaches and players were on board with the new policy, regarding it as a way to get past the controversy generated by the protests and focus on football and community activism off the field.

Concerns about the New Policy

In the days after the NFL announced the new policy, many NFL coaches and players affirmed their intention to follow the new rules, but also underscored their continued support for the players' rights to protest for social justice.

In an interview, Dirk Koetter, the head coach of the Tampa Bay Buccaneers, underscored the importance of addressing the policy with his players. "It's important to continue to work with the players. If you remember, I really don't think this started out as a national anthem issue. That's not what the protest is about. Again, we have a policy now, and we'll work through that policy and we'll do what we're supposed to do within that policy" (ESPN 2018).

Many NFL players took issue with the new policy, viewing it as a violation of their constitutional right to free speech and an attempt by the league to stifle their attempts to address social injustice. Others criticized the NFL for capitulating to political pressures, especially President Trump's sharp criticism of the players.

Artie Burns, a cornerback for the Pittsburgh Steelers, argued that the new policy was not a viable solution. He predicted it would be divisive and stigmatize players who stayed in the locker room during the anthem. "I feel like it's another topic to get everybody against each other. I hate that we have to go down this route but it is what it is. . . . [Staying in the locker room] makes you look bad. The whole team is out there and you come jogging out (and people say) 'Oh, he's the guy that's (protesting).' Who wants to go through that? That's humiliating as a person" (ESPN 2018).

The National Football League Players Association (NFLPA) came out against the policy, noting that it had been formulated without input from the union and contradicted statements made by NFL ownership and league officials. On July 10, the NFLPA filed a grievance challenging the policy. "The union's claim is that this new policy, imposed by the NFL's governing body without consultation with the NFLPA, is inconsistent with the collective bargaining agreement and infringes on player's right," the union explained on Twitter (NFLPA 2018).

Reconsidering the New Policy

In July 2018, a copy of the Miami Dolphins' revised disciplinary guidelines leaked to the press, sparking outrage. According the document, participating in player protests during the national anthem was classified in the same "conduct detrimental to the club" category as gambling, drug possession, or breaking curfew. Discipline for players who protested during the anthem could be a suspension for up to four games without pay (Lockhart, 2018).

Although the Dolphins stated the guidelines were only a placeholder and no final decisions on disciplinary actions for NFL protests had been made, the damage was done. Within hours, the NFL and the NFLPA issued a joint statement on pausing the new policy and reopening discussions on a more effective way to address NFL player protests.

"The NFL and NFLPA, through recent discussions, have been working on a resolution to the anthem issue. In order to allow this constructive dialogue to continue, we have come to a standstill agreement on the NFLPA's grievance and on the NFL's anthem policy. No new rules relating to the anthem will be issued or enforced for the next several weeks while these confidential discussions are ongoing" (NFLPA 2018).

Further Reading

ESPN. 2018. "NFL Players, Coaches, and Owners React to National Anthem Policy." *ESPN*, May 24, 2018. http://www.espn.com/blo/nflnation/post/_/id/275970/players-coaches-and-owners-react-to-the-national-anthem-policy

Glauber, Bob. 2018. "Jets' Chairman Christopher Johnson Backs Players' Right to Protest." *Newsday*, May 23, 2018. https://www.newsday.com/sports/football/jets/national-anthem-christopher-johnson-fines-1.18700702

Gleeson, Scott. 2017. "Roger Goodell Wants NFL to Move Past Protests, Says Fans Come to Games to 'Have Fun'." *USA Today*, November 9, 2017. https://www.usatoday.com/story/sports/nfl/2017/11/09/roger-goodell-wants-nfl-move-past-anthem-protests-says-fans-come-games-to-have-fun/848325001/

Goodell, Roger. 2018. "Roger Goodell's Statement on National Anthem Policy." NFL.com, May 23, 2018. http://www.nfl.com/news/story/0ap3000000933962/article/roger-goodells-statement-on-national-anthem-policy

Jacksonville Jaguars (@Jaguars). 2018. Twitter, May 23, 2018. https://twitter.com/Jaguars/status/999356965494108163

Lockhart, P. R. 2018. "The Miami Dolphins Acted on the NFL's Anthem Policy. The League Was Unprepared for the Backlash." *Vox*, July 20, 2018. https://www.vox.com/identities/2018/7/20/17596268/nfl-anthem-policy-miami-dolphins-kneeling-protest-donald-trump

National Football League. 2018. "Donald Trump: NFL Did the 'Right Thing' with Anthem Policy." NFL.com, May 24, 2018. http://www.nfl.com/news/story/0ap3000000934197/article/donald-trump-nfl-did-right-thing-with-anthem-policy

NFL Players Association (@NFLPA). 2018. Twitter, July 10, 2018. https://twitter.com/NFLPA/status/1016707389372936199

NFL Players Association. 2018. NFLPA.com, July 20, 2018. https://www.nflpa.com/news/joint-statement-on-anthem-policy

The White House Cancels Its Super Bowl Championship Celebration (2018)

On February 4, 2018, the Philadelphia Eagles beat the New England Patriots in Super Bowl LII at U.S. Bank Stadium in Minneapolis, Minnesota. It was the first Super Bowl victory for the Eagles and the team's fourth NFL championship in its history. One of the last major events on the Eagles off-season schedule to commemorate the team's Super Bowl victory was the traditional White House visit, scheduled for June 5. However, when the White House withdrew the invitation the day before the event and President Donald Trump questioned the patriotism of the players, many commentators, players, and fans began to rethink the value of the tradition itself.

The History of White House Visits and Sports Teams

The connection between the White House and sports leagues has a long history. The first time an American sports team visited the White House was August 30, 1865, when President Andrew Johnson hosted the Brooklyn Atlantics and the Washington Nationals, two amateur baseball clubs, to an event in their honor. The 1924 Washington Senators was the first World Series championship team to be honored at the White House. By the mid-twentieth century, NFL teams frequently received invitations to the White House. President Jimmy Carter became the first president to honor the Super Bowl champion with a White House ceremony when he invited the Pittsburgh Steelers in February 1980.

During the administration of Ronald Reagan, the informal tradition of inviting sports champions was established. Today, about a dozen professional and major college teams are invited per year. This includes not only teams from major professional leagues but also NCAA Division I champions and Olympic and Paralympic medal-winning athletes.

Along with a ceremony at the White House, teams developed a tradition of performing community service in the Washington, D.C., area during their visit. Some players sat with wounded soldiers at hospitals, while others held youth fitness clinics or mentored young athletes. A number of teams donated needed equipment to high school sports teams in underserved communities.

The Context for the White House Visit

Around the time of the Eagles' scheduled White House visit, tensions between President Trump and NFL players were strained. Just a few weeks before, the NFL owners announced a new national anthem policy, meant to stop NFL players from protesting during the playing of the national anthem. The new policy required players and team personnel to stand—not take a knee or sit on the bench—if they were on the field during the anthem. However, players or team personnel could choose to stay in the locker room during the anthem. The NFL could fine any team found to be in violation of the policy. Many players throughout the league objected to the change, viewing it as giving in to increasing political pressure from President Trump and NFL Commissioner Roger Goodell and an attempt by the owners to curtail the civil rights of NFL players.

In a tweet later that day, Philadelphia Eagles defensive end Chris Long argued owners had voted for the new policy because of pressure from President Trump and suggested they were more concerned about business than players. "This is a fear of a diminished bottom line," he posted. "It's also a fear of a president turning his base against a corporation. This isn't patriotism. Don't get it confused. These owners don't love America more than the players demonstrating and taking real action to improve it" (@JOEL9ONE May 23, 2018).

Philadelphia Eagles team owner Jeff Lurie reaffirmed the importance of his players' social justice activism and community involvement. "In this great country of ours, there are so many people who are hurting and marginalized, which is why I am proud of our players for continuously working to influence positive change," he maintained in a statement. "Their words and actions have demonstrated not only that they have a great deal of respect for our country, but also that they are committed to finding productive ways to fight social injustice, poverty and other societal issues that are important to all of us. We must continue to work together in creative and dynamic ways to make our communities stronger and better with equal opportunities for all" (Zangaro 2018).

President Trump, however, supported the new policy. "I think that's good," he remarked. "I don't think people should be staying in locker rooms but I still think it's good, you have to stand proudly for the national anthem. Or you shouldn't be playing, you shouldn't be there. Maybe you shouldn't be in the country. You have to stand proudly for the national anthem and the NFL owners did the right thing if that's what they've done" (NFL.com 2018).

The Decision

As the scheduled White House visit approached, Eagles players and team officials debated how the team should handle it. Several players objected to Trump's divisive rhetoric and announced they would not attend. Some players supported the idea of a team trip with only those comfortable with the White House event attending while everyone else participated in community service or sightseeing. In the end, Lurie decided to send a group of 10 players, including Super Bowl MVP Nick Foles, to the White House.

On June 4, the day before the scheduled visit, the White House cancelled. In a statement, the president blamed the cancellation on what he said was the team's lack of patriotism. "[The Philadelphia Eagles] disagree with their president because he insists that they proudly stand for the National Anthem, hand on heart, in honor of the great men and women of our military and the people of our country. The Eagles wanted to send a smaller delegation, but the 1,000 fans planning to attend deserve better" (Trump 2018).

The Aftermath

The day of the cancellation, the Philadelphia Eagles released a tweet downplaying the incident. "It has been incredibly thrilling to celebrate our first Super Bowl championship. Watching the entire Eagles community come together has been an inspiration. We are truly grateful for all the support we have received and are looking forward to continuing our preparations for the 2018 season" (@Eagles June 4, 2018).

Eagles player Malcolm Jenkins took issue with Trump's characterization of Eagles players as unpatriotic. "Simply google: 'How many Philadelphia Eagles knelt during the anthem this season?' and you find the answer is zero," he tweeted. "A similar google search will show you how many great things the players on this team are doing and continue to do on a daily basis. Instead the decision was made to lie, and paint the picture that these players are anti-America, anti-flag, and anti-military" (@MalcolmJenkins June 5, 2018).

The NFL Players Association (NFLPA) also emphasized the team's community service and patriotism. "Our union is disappointed in the decision by the White House to disinvite players from the Philadelphia Eagles from being recognized and celebrated by all Americans for their accomplishment," the statement read. "This decision by the White house has led to the cancellation of several player-led community service events for young people in the Washington, DC, area. NFL players love their country, support our troops, give back to our communities and strive to make America a better place" (NFLPA 2018).

Further Reading

Jenkins, Malcolm (@MalcolmJenkins). 2018. Twitter, June 5, 2018. https://twitter.com/MalcolmJenkins/status/1004049505812172800

Long, Chris (@JOEL9ONE). 2018. Twitter, May 23, 2018. https://twitter.com/JOEL9ONE/status/999408653445795840

Neumann, Thomas. 2016. "Why White House Visits by Champions Are a U.S. Tradition." ESPN, March 1, 2016. http://www.espn.com/college-football/story/_/id/14870667/how-white-house-visits-championship-teams-became-american-tradition

National Football League. 2018. "Donald Trump: NFL Did the 'Right Thing' with Anthem Policy." NFL.com, May 24, 2018. http://www.nfl.com/news/story/0ap3000000934197/article/donald-trump-nfl-did-right-thing-with-anthem-policy

NFL Players Association. 2018. "NFLPA Statement on Philadelphia Eagles White House Visit." NFLPA, June 5, 2018. https://www.nflpa.com/news/nflpa-statement-on-philadelphia-eagles-white-house-visit

Philadelphia Eagles. 2018. Twitter, June 4, 2018. https://twitter.com/Eagles/status/1003829058214514688/photo/1

Trump, Donald. 2018. "Statement by the President," June 4, 2018. https://www.whitehouse.gov/briefings-statements/statement-by-the-president-2/

Zangaro, Dave. 2018. "Jeff Lurie Releases Statement in Light of NFL's National Anthem Policy." *NBC Sports*, May 23, 2018. https://www.nbcsports.com/philadelphia/eagles/jeff-lurie-releases-statement-nfl-national-anthem-policy

CHAPTER THREE

Impacts of the NFL National Anthem Protests

This section examines the impact of the National Football League players' protests during the national anthem on U.S. life and culture, including changes in the NFL and in national politics, as well as renewed debates about patriotism, First Amendment rights, police brutality, and racism.

NFL Protests Impact Corporate Sponsors

After President Donald Trump denounced NFL players protesting racial inequality and police brutality by taking a knee during the national anthem in September 2017, the controversy over the NFL protests exploded. Protest supporters objected to the president's criticism, seeing it as a cynical way to rally his political base. They argued players had a constitutional right to express their opinions on social injustice issues. To these supporters, peacefully demonstrating for action against injustice was patriotic because it exercised the right to free speech, a core American value. However, many Americans opposed the protests, taking the same stand as the president that during national anthem was not the right time to protest social justice issues. They thought the NFL should have a tighter policy on national anthem protests, imposing penalties on those who participated.

The backlash affected the NFL's corporate sponsors because critics of the protests organized sponsor boycotts. These boycotts hurt product sales and damaged their image with more conservative fans. Corporate sponsors who made their opposition to the NFL protests clear experienced counterattacks, mainly through criticism on social media.

The NFL protests led a number of corporations to reevaluate sponsoring the league or its players. It also led to a larger debate over how corporations should handle controversies that could alienate customers.

The Financial Value of Corporate Sponsorships

Many top U.S. corporations continued to invest in the league, including Anheuser Busch, Nike, FedEx, Ford Motor Company, Verizon, Visa, and Microsoft. According to the International Evaluation Group Sponsorship Report, NFL corporate sponsors spent $1.32 billion on the league and its individual teams during the 2017–2018 season, which the league profits from (IEG, 2018). That figure signaled a 5.9 percent increase in sponsorship revenue compared to the 2016–2017 season (IEG, 2018).

Corporate sponsors establish a marketing relationship with the league and gain access to NFL fans. In the United States, 65 percent of adults watch NFL games on TV and online, with 74 percent of American men tuning in (Global Web Index 2015). That translates into profit for corporate sponsors. "NFL fans in the U.S. are 20% more likely than average to say they tend to buy brands they see being advertised" (Global Web Index, 2015). The NFL attracts sponsors selling food, beverages, music, film, entertainment, cars, and technology.

When corporations become official NFL sponsors, their image becomes associated with the goals, values, and vision of the league. Over the years, the NFL carefully created a conservative, patriotic image. Therefore, when critics of the protest, especially President Trump, attacked NFL players for taking a knee or raising a fist during the national anthem, the league's official corporate sponsors also came under scrutiny.

The Case of Papa John's Pizza

Founded in 1984, Papa John's Pizza is a large and popular pizza takeout and delivery franchise based in the United States. In January 2010, the company announced its role as official pizza sponsor of the NFL and Super Bowl XLIV. "Companies and brands associate with the NFL and the Super Bowl because they are committed to a quality and leadership position," stated Andrew Varga, chief marketing officer for Papa John's. "This is an important marketing partnership for Papa John's, as there is no better combination in our industry than pizza and NFL football" (Papa John's 2010).

Papa John's prominently featured its sponsorship of the NFL in its marketing campaigns. Peyton Manning, a former NFL quarterback, became a spokesperson for the brand. For several years, he appeared in TV advertisements alongside John Schnatter, Papa John's CEO and founder.

In late 2017, as the controversy over NFL national anthem protests escalated, the relationship between the NFL and Papa John's grew strained. In November 2017, the company blamed the NFL protest controversy for its slow sales growth. "The NFL has hurt us," stated Schnatter. "And more importantly, by not resolving the current debacle to the player and owners' satisfaction, NFL leadership has hurt Papa John's shareholders. Let me explain. The NFL has been a long and valued partner over the years, but we are certainly disappointed that the NFL and its leadership did not resolve the ongoing situation to the satisfaction of all parties long ago" (Yahoo Finance 2017).

Schnatter's comments pulled the company into the debate over the NFL anthem protests. Critics of the demonstrations pointed to Schnatter's statement as evidence that the player protests harmed both the image and the bottom line of the NFL. However, when the *Daily Stormer*, a white supremacist publication, suggested the pizza chain should be the official pizza of the alt-right because of its sharp criticism of the NFL protests, Papa John's responded quickly to the growing public relations controversy.

"The statements made on our earnings call were describing the factors that impact our business and we sincerely apologize to anyone that thought they were divisive. That was definitely not our intention. We believe in the right to protest inequality and support the players' movement to create a new platform for change. We also believe together, as Americans, we should honor our anthem. There is a way to do both. We will work with the players and league to find a positive way forward. Open to ideas from all. Except neo-Nazis— [emoji of middle finger] those guys" (@PapaJohns November 14, 2017).

However, the damage was done. Many NFL fans saw Schnatter's comments as dishonest, an attempt to blame NFL player protesters for his company's poor performance. Schnatter, a conservative and a vocal Trump supporter, became a controversial figure. Over the following weeks, the company's stock value declined, and sales continued to slump. In December 2017, Papa John's announced that Schnatter would step down as CEO. In February 2018, the NFL and Papa John's said the company was bowing out of its NFL sponsorship deal. Instead, Pizza Hut became the official pizza sponsor for the NFL.

The Lesson for Other Corporate Sponsors

The Papa John's controversy was a cautionary tale for corporate sponsors in general. By diving into a contentious issue, Papa John's drew attention away from their product and alienated many existing and potential customers. In addition, the company was perceived to be playing both sides of the issue, and generating resentment from both sides in the process.

In the following months, other corporate sponsors of the NFL managed to avoid the mistakes made by Papa John's. Most sponsors did not explicitly take sides, but a few defended the constitutional rights of all Americans—including NFL players—to protest against social injustice.

The Case of Nike

On the 30th anniversary of the company's iconic "just do it" advertising campaign, Nike, an NFL sponsor, decided to go against conventional wisdom and make a controversial statement. On September 3, 2018, Nike launched a new ad campaign featuring Colin Kaepernick, the former San Francisco 49ers quarterback who had initiated the NFL protest movement in 2016. In the ad, the message "Believe in something. Even if it means sacrificing everything. Just do it," accompanies a close-up of Kaepernick's face. Nike plans on developing a line of apparel and shoes featuring Kaepernick.

In response to the Kaepernick ad campaign, critics of the NFL protests spoke out. Many posted their disappointment on social media and called for a boycott of Nike products. A few outraged people posted videos of themselves burning Nike shoes and apparel in protest.

However, many business and sports analysts praised the move, pointing out that Nike's demographic is young, trendy, and urban—and also supportive of the protests in general. "It's an interesting decision for Nike," maintained Frank Schwab. "No other athlete produces the same emotional response than Kaepernick. Some will rip Nike and claim they'll never buy their products again. Others who support Kaepernick will gladly shift their dollars to Nike for its support of the former San Francisco 49ers quarterback, who is viewed as a hero to many for standing up for social issues even if it meant the NFL ultimately would freeze him out. If Nike wanted the maximum attention possible for its new advertising campaign, mission accomplished" (Schwab 2018).

Trump's criticism of the Nike campaign was pronounced. He called it a "a terrible message." He added, "As much as I disagree with the Colin Kaepernick endorsement, in another way—I mean, I wouldn't have done it. In another way, it is what the country is all about, that you have certain freedoms to do things that other people think you shouldn't do, but I am personally on another side of it" (Coglianese and Enjeti 2018).

On September 5, Trump criticized Nike's stance. "Just like the NFL, whose ratings have gone WAY DOWN, Nike is getting absolutely killed with anger and boycotts. I wonder if they had any idea that it would be this way? As far as the NFL is concerned, I just find it hard to watch, and always will, until they stand for the FLAG!" (@realDonaldTrump September 5, 2018).

Further Reading

Coglianese, Vince, and Saagar Enjeti. 2018. "Trump Critical, but Says Nike's Kaepernick Deal Is 'What This Country Is All about'." *Daily Caller*, September 4, 2018. https://dailycaller.com/2018/09/04/trump-interview-nike-kaepernick-deal/

Global Web Index. 2015. "NFL Fans: Polling the Demographics, Attitudes and Digital Behaviors of NFL Fans." https://cdn2.hubspot.net/hub/304927/file-2395712248-pdf/Reports/NFL_Fans_Audience_Report_Q1_2015.pdf?submissionGuid=e7c143b7-d707-41eb-b9ca-24d2264b2766

IEG. 2018. "NFL Sponsorship Revenue Totals $1.32 Billion in 2017-2018 Season." *IEG Sponsorship Report*, January 29, 2018. http://www.sponsorship.com/Report/2018/01/29/NFL-Sponsorship-Revenue-Totals-$1-32-Billion-In-20.aspx

Papa John's. 2010. "Papa John's Takes the Field as Official Pizza Sponsor of the NFL and Super Bowl XLIV." January 10, 2010. http://ir.papajohns.com/news-releases/news-release-details/papa-johns-takes-field-official-pizza-sponsor-nfl-and-super-bowl

Papa John's (@PapaJohns). 2017. Twitter, November 14, 2017. https://twitter.com/PapaJohns/status/930588793635209216

Rovell, Darren. 2017. "Papa John's Says Anthem Protests Are Hurting Deal with the NFL." *Sports Illustrated*, November 1, 2017. http://www.espn.com/nfl/story/_/id/21250448/nfl-sponsor-papa-john-not-happy-anthem-protests

Schwab, Frank. 2018. "Nike Makes Colin Kaepernick the Face of 'Just Do It' 30th Anniversary Campaign." *Yahoo Sports,* September 4, 2018. https://sports.yahoo.com/nike-makes-colin-kaepernick-face-just-30th-anniversary-campaign-200029766.html

Taylor, Kate, and Dennis Green. 2017. "Here's How All of the NFL's Sponsors Have Responded to Backlash over Players' National Anthem Protests." *Business Insider*, November 7, 2017. https://www.businessinsider.com/nfl-protests-how-brands-have-responded-2017-11

Trump, Donald (@realDonaldTrump). Twitter, September 5, 2018. https://twitter.com/realDonaldTrump/status/1037334510159966214

Yahoo. 2017. "Edited Transcript of PZZA Earnings Conference Call or Presentation 1-Nov-2017 2:00 pm GMT." *Yahoo Finance*, November 2, 2017. https://finance.yahoo.com/news/edited-transcript-pzza-earnings-conference-120053736.html

NFL Protests Affect National Politics

At a rally on September 22, 2017, President Donald Trump responded to NFL players who were taking a knee during the national anthem to protest racial inequality and police brutality, attacking them as unpatriotic and disrespectful and urging NFL owners to fire them if they continued. Trump's condemnation inspired loud cheers from his supporters. From then on, Trump regularly took to social media to criticize the NFL protests, the players who participated in the demonstrations, the league itself, and team owners, apparently seeing the issue as a political winner for him.

As Trump exploited the issue, the controversy also led to larger conversations about racial inequality, police brutality, free speech in the workplace, and the meaning of patriotism itself. In the process, debates over these issues have exposed and exacerbated racial and political tensions in the United States. The impact of the NFL protests on U.S. politics has been profound, widening a partisan divide during the Trump administration.

Politicians Respond

Other political figures reacted to Trump's criticism of NFL players. Some conservative lawmakers defended the protests. For example, the late Republican Senator John McCain defended the players' right to free speech.

Other conservatives strongly opposed the protests. Republican Congressman Clay Higgins threatened to boycott the NFL. "My Sundays have a lot more Harley-Davidson time now," he remarked in a radio interview. "Unless and until the NFL makes a bold stance against the appalling disrespect of our national anthem, the NFL is dead to me" (Connelly 2017).

New York Congressman Peter King criticized New York Jets owner Christopher Johnson for offering to pay fines associated with the protests. "Would he support all player protests?" King asked on Twitter. "Would he pay fines of players giving Nazi salutes or spew racism?" (@RepPeteKing May 26, 2018).

Many Democrats supported the protests and saw an opportunity to criticize the president for using the issue to divide the American people and distract from other issues, such as the ineffective response to the devastation wrought by Hurricane Maria in Puerto Rico in September 2017 and threats of aggression from North Korea. However, the Democratic leadership in the House and Senate largely remained silent on the issue.

That changed when a video was released in August 2018 by Texas Senate Democratic candidate Beto O'Rourke that got more than a million views. O'Rourke strongly defended the protests as standing for the right to free speech and put them in the context of the Civil Rights struggles of the 1960s. O'Rourke's opponent, incumbent Senator Ted Cruz, took the opportunity to make his opposition to the NFL protests a campaign issue in the Texas Senate race.

The Political Debate over Patriotism

In Trump's attacks on players who took a knee during the national anthem, he painted the protests as unpatriotic—a perception many Americans shared.

"That there are legitimate grounds for protest is incontrovertible," argued conservative journalist Paul Jenkins. "This nation has not always done right by its minorities. Even given that, why is it acceptable for multimillionaire players and coaches and team owners to denigrate the very people who served and sacrificed to protect their right to protest injustice?" (Jenkins 2017).

Trump perceived the frustration of his base and fed the controversy. When some NFL players protested at the start of the 2018 season, Trump objected. Such attacks appealed to his base. Many Trump supporters seemed to think the media and the culture at large ignored their opinions. They were also drawn to Trump's willingness to take on America's favorite sport. Trump's understanding of his base supporters' views on patriotism allowed him to exploit the NFL anthem protests to his political advantage.

Critics of the president questioned his vocal defense of patriotism on the football field while his own background, actions, and political policies violated American ideals. They pointed to his not serving in the Vietnam war, his questionable associations with Mafia figures and corrupt foreign governments as a real-estate developer, his praise for brutal dictators like Vladimir Putin, and his cynical efforts to stoke racial and political divisions as president. Trump's attacks on the free speech of players—who were exercising their constitutional right to protest racial inequality and police brutality—as well as his calls to NFL officials and team owners to limit these rights also raised questions about the authenticity of the president's patriotic image.

Some critics of the president argued the NFL players protesting during the national anthem embodied the true meaning of patriotism. Political commentator Conor Friedersdorf noted, "The president's deft manipulation of that misperception [that the protesters are anti-flag] is especially frustrating for Americans whose patriotism is properly grounded in the core values of the Founding. Many regard the flag as a symbol of those values, and therefore believe that the protesting NFL players have a far greater claim to the flag than does the president—that while he abuses his position by pressuring a private enterprise to punish its employees for their political speech, the NFL players, kneeling together in public protest of *what they believe to be unjust killings,* are acting in ways that have parallels to the Founders. That is, they are pledging their honor and risking their fortunes in political protest in what they see as a government that is failing to secure the rights of Americans, and failing in particular *to protect their lives and liberty*" (Friedersdorf 2018).

The Controversy as Distraction

Many commentators argued that Trump's attacks on NFL protesters served as an easy distraction from a myriad of other controversial issues, particularly the investigation into Russian interference into the 2016 presidential election. They claimed the media spent more time covering Trump's tweets on the NFL protests or the league's national anthem policy than it did on other potentially damaging issues and emerging scandals. The controversy over the NFL protests—and the media's coverage of it—were also fodder for his base.

Many critics found Trump's cynical use of patriotism for political advantage deplorable. For example, journalist Jonathan Chait commented, "I happen to find a lot to admire in patriotism. At its best, it can summon our highest ideals and demand that we live up to them—think Martin Luther King reciting the Declaration of Independence—and help an often-divided people see our commonality. At its worst, patriotism can devolve into my-country-right-or-wrong nationalism that allows us to overlook our failings. What is so wrong about Trump is that even this second, lower version of patriotism is a bar he fails to clear" (Chait 2018).

Polls Confirm the Partisan Divide

Public opinion polls about the protests revealed the extent of the partisan divide. A May 2018 Morning Consult poll showed that 83 percent of Republicans opposed NFL players kneeling during the national anthem, while 43 percent of Independents and 25 percent of Democrats opposed the player protests (Sabin 2018). Between September 2017 and May 2018, Republican opposition to the protests jumped from 77 percent to 83 percent, reflecting a much more polarized position than either Independents or Democrats who responded to the poll. There was also a partisan divide over how Trump treated African American athletes in general. An August 2018 CBS/YouGov poll reported that 65 percent of Republicans approved of Trump's attitude toward African American athletes, while only 32 percent of all Americans approved (Salvanto 2018).

With public opinion on Trump's handling of racial issues split along partisan lines, political analysts argued that Trump was using the NFL protests to appeal his Republican base, which is largely white and older, at the expense of Democratic voters, who tend to be younger and more diverse.

The Political Value of the Culture War

Trump's attacks on protesting NFL players were only one element of his larger cultural crusade. Other aspects included Trump's stricter immigration policies, his defense of Confederate statues in public places, his labeling of the mainstream media as "fake news," and his tendency to insult and demean celebrities, athletes, and other public figures who criticized him. Trump's attack on the establishment—political and cultural—appealed to a large section of society who advocated a radical change in American society.

"There mere act of stirring outrage lets the country know the multicultural left is not calling the shots," political analyst Bill Scher noted. "If 'social justice warriors' rage online and TV talking heads sputter, then as far as [Trump] and his #MAGA fans are concerned: Mission Accomplished" (Scher 2017).

Trump's culture war may not attract new supporters, but analysts maintain it effectively rallies his political base. Stoking racial and partisan divisions reaped political benefits during the presidential campaign; analysts expected that it would once again attract the electoral support that Trump and Republicans needed in the months before the all-important 2018 midterm elections—a contest that would determine control over the U.S. House and Senate. Without an enthusiastic base, Republicans were at risk of losing the majority in both houses, which could lead to obstruction of Republican policies, in-depth investigations into alleged Trump administration corruption, mismanagement, and relationships with foreign governments, and even impeachment of the president if warranted.

Further Reading

Chait, Jonathan. 2018. "Most Unpatriotic President Ever Says Kneeling NFL Players 'Shouldn't Be in the Country'." *New York Magazine*, May 24, 2018. http://nymag.com/daily/intelligencer/2018/05/trump-is-the-least-patriotic -american-president-ever.html

Connelly, Griffin. 2017. "Lawmakers Join the Battle over NFL Protests." *Roll Call*, September 27, 2017. https://www.rollcall.com/news/politics/lawmakers -stand-nfl-protests-presidents-response

Friedersdorf, Conor. 2018. "How NFL Players Can Avoid Playing into Trump's Hands." *The Atlantic*, July 21, 2018. https://www.theatlantic.com/politics/archive/2018/07/the-nfl-controversys-likely-return/565661/

Jenkins, Paul. 2017. "NFL Players' Protest Is an Insult, Period." *Anchorage Daily News*, September 29, 2017. https://www.adn.com/opinions/2017/09/29/nfl-players-protest-is-an-insult-period/

King, Pete (@RepPeteKing). 2018. Twitter, May 26, 2018. https://twitter.com/RepPeteKing/status/1000371463705235456

Sabin, Sam. 2018. "NFL's National Anthem Policy Draws Support from 53% of U.S. Adults in One Poll." *Morning Consult*, May 31, 2018. https://morningconsult.com/2018/05/31/nfls-national-anthem-policy-draws-support-us-adults-poll/https://morningconsult.com/2018/05/31/nfls-national-anthem-policy-draws-support-us-adults-poll/

Salvanto, Anthony. 2018. "Poll: One Year after Charlottesville, Majority of Americans See Racial Tensions on the Rise." *CBS News*, August 12, 2018. https://www.cbsnews.com/news/poll-one-year-after-charlottesville-americans-see-racial-tensions-on-increase/

Scher, Bill. 2017. "The Culture War President." *Politico*, September 27, 2017. https://www.politico.com/magazine/story/2017/09/27/trump-culture-war-215653

Trump, Donald (@realDonaldTrump). 2018. Twitter, August 10, 2018. https://twitter.com/realDonaldTrump/status/1027892043908046849

Impact on Other Sports Leagues

The player protests during the 2016 NFL season had a big impact on the league in light of its conservative and patriotic image. But the resulting national debate affected other American professional sports leagues as well.

The National Basketball Association

In the National Basketball Association (NBA), the policy on the national anthem is much more restrictive than the NFL's policy. "Players, coaches, and trainers are to stand and line up in a dignified posture along the sidelines or on the foul line during the playing of the national anthem" (Seifert 2018). However, the NBA has not faced criticism as severe as that experienced by the NFL over the issue of player protests.

One of the main reasons for that is the way the NBA values the players' voices on social justice issues. Over the past few years, NBA players have made their voices heard in a number of different ways. In 2014, Cleveland Cavaliers superstar LeBron James and a group of NBA players wore "I Can't Breathe" T-shirts during warm-ups to protest the death of Eric Garner, an African

American, at the hands of police in Staten Island, New York. Several NBA players, including Steph Curry, Dwyane Wade, Chris Paul, and LeBron James, spoke out on social justice issues in public forums, such as the annual ESPYs award ceremony. Many NBA players also voiced their strong support for Colin Kaepernick, the NFL star quarterback who had been the first to take a knee during the national anthem, on social media and to the press.

NBA teams not only support their players but also share their social justice concerns. In the aftermath of controversial police shootings, teams released statements criticizing police mistreatment of African Americans. Criminal justice reform, poverty, systematic racial inequality, and education are several issues NBA teams have addressed in their communities. As one commentator noted, "Players don't need to kneel in protest if the teams are out there making the same points they want to make about the same problems" (Graziano 2018).

For NBA players, taking a knee is a symbolic action, while actually making an impact on one's community through concrete action is more effective in the long run. "I think a lot has been said about how the NBA guys—and definitely the case in the NFL too—are actually doing stuff on the back end and using their platforms and connections and their networks and money to actually (make a difference)," said Curry. "It feels good to have that kind of impact, to actually help create change in the ways that you can. . . . The attention needs to be on that, and how that's impacting the community as opposed to 130 guys kneeling in the NFL. That's great, but this is the stuff that matters and this is the stuff that can actually move the needle when it comes to impacting the next generation" (Amick 2017). As James argued, "My voice and what I do in my community is more powerful than getting on a knee" (Amick 2017).

The league hasn't always been so progressive on social justice protests. In 1996, Denver Nuggets player Mahmoud Abdul-Rauf was suspended for one game when he refused to stand for the national anthem before a game. Abdul-Rauf and then NBA Commissioner David Stern worked out a compromise that allowed him to stand and pray silently during that time.

The Women's National Basketball Association

The Women's National Basketball Association (WNBA) rule on the national anthem is identical to the NBA rule. Like the NBA, the WNBA has worked to support its players' right to free speech and community activism, and it shares its social justice concerns. "This [social and political engagement] is very much encoded, I think, in the DNA of the WNBA," said Lisa Borders, WNBA president (Katz 2018).

On social issues, the league has been at the forefront of advocating for social change, especially racial equality and LGBT rights. In summer 2016, before the NFL's Colin Kaepernick took a knee, WNBA teams spoke to the press and raised awareness at games and on social media about police brutality after the killings of two African American men, Alton Sterling and Philando Castile, by police officers. On July 9, players of the Minnesota Lynx held a press conference to discuss police brutality following the killing of Castile in St. Paul. That same month, players from the Lynx, New York Liberty, and Phoenix Mercury wore Black Lives Matter T-shirts during warm-ups. The WNBA fined all three teams $5,000 and each player $500; however, the league later rescinded the fines after players and the public complained.

The NFL protests inspired some WNBA players to protest during the national anthem. In September 2016, the entire Indiana Fever team and two Phoenix Mercury players (Mistie Bass and Kelsey Bone) took a knee on the basketball court before a WNBA playoff game. The league did not penalize the protesting players. During the WNBA Finals that same year, the Los Angeles Sparks remained in the locker room during the national anthem, fully supported by team ownership and fans.

Major League Baseball

According to an MLB spokesperson, there are no documented rules about protesting during the national anthem. "While this is not a league rule, the playing of the national anthems of the United States and Canada remains an important tradition that has great meaning to our fans" (Seifert 2018).

Throughout 2016, no MLB players protested during the national anthem. When asked about the issue, Baltimore Orioles all-star centerfielder Adam Jones pointed to the low number of African American players in baseball as the central reason. "We already have two strikes against us already," he asserted, "so you might as well not kick yourself out of the game. In football, you can't kick them out. You need those players. In baseball, they don't need us. Baseball is a white man's sport" (Nightengale 2016).

Jones's comments shone a light on the way many African American baseball players felt about making their voices heard on issues of racial inequality and police brutality. In 2018, African Americans comprised 8.4 percent of MLB rosters, while nearly 70 percent of NFL players were African American. To many observers, the disparity between the two leagues implies that black MLB players who protest during the national anthem may not have the same level of support among teammates as NFL players. Furthermore, baseball culture has historically required players to put their political opinions aside in favor of a show of unity and relieving any clubhouse tensions that could hurt the team's performance on the field.

The first—and only—MLB player to kneel during the national anthem was Oakland Athletics rookie catcher Bruce Maxwell, the son of an Army veteran, who knelt in September 2017. "I'm kneeling for the people who don't have a voice," he explained after the game. His protest came one day after President Donald Trump attacked NFL protesters as unpatriotic and disrespectful during a political rally in Alabama on September 22, 2017.

The MLB released a statement on the Maxwell protest: "Major League Baseball has a longstanding tradition of honoring our nation prior to the start of our games. We also respect that each of our players is an individual with his own background, perspectives and opinions. We believe that our game will continue to bring our fans, their communities, and our players together" (MLB 2017).

Maxwell continued to take a knee before every game for the rest of the 2017 season, but he decided to end his protest before the 2018 regular season, saying, "The purpose of the gesture was to raise awareness of social issues affecting our country, and while I'm looking forward to a society that is inclusive, empathetic, and a welcoming place, I will not continue the symbolic gesture of taking a knee during our national anthem this season" (Lee 2018).

The National Hockey League

Like the MLB, the National Hockey League (NHL) has not codified any specific rule or policy on the national anthem. The only NHL player to protest during the 2017–2018 season was Tampa Bay Lightning forward J. T. Brown, only one of about 30 black players in the league. Before a game in October 2017, Brown raised one fist in the air during "The Star-Spangled Banner" to protest racial inequality and police brutality.

NHL commissioner Gary Bettman asserted that the league would not be enacting a specific rule on the matter. "Our players are basically doing what they believe is correct and that is giving our fans and giving their teams focus right on the game itself. Before the game, after the game, on their time off we encourage them to be as socially active and involved as they'd like to be . . . and exercise their political choice" (Schlager 2018).

The U.S. Soccer Federation and Major League Soccer

In September 2016, professional soccer player Megan Rapinoe attracted international attention when she began kneeling during the playing of the national anthem before matches. As she explained, "I haven't experienced over-policing, racial profiling, police brutality or the sight of a family member's body lying dead in the street. But I cannot stand idly by while there are people in this country who have had to deal with this kind of heartache. There is no perfect way to protest. I know that nothing I do will take away the pain of these families. But I feel in my heart it is right to continue to kneel during the national anthem, and I will do whatever I can to be part of the solution" (Rapinoe 2016).

The controversy over Rapinoe's protest led the U.S. Soccer Federation to change its policy on the matter in February 2017. The revised policy required players to "stand respectfully" during the playing of the national anthem at any Federation event.

In contrast to the U.S. Soccer Federation, Major League Soccer released a statement supporting its players' right to express their beliefs. Many commentators pointed out that the difference in MLS and USSF policies stems from distinction regarding playing for club or playing for country.

Further Reading

Amick, Sam. 2017. "Why You Shouldn't Expect NBA Players to Kneel for the National Anthem." *USA Today*, October 17, 2017. https://www.usatoday.com/story/sports/nba/2017/10/17/nba-players-take-action-than-take-knee-national-anthem-protest/771401001/

Begley, Ian. 2017. "Adam Silver Says Players Know Respecting the Flag Is Important." ESPN, September 29, 2017. http://www.espn.com/nba/story/_/id/20853206/nba-commissioner-adam-silver-expects-players-stand-national-anthem

Graziano, Dan. 2018. "Why the NFL Is Light Years behind the NBA on Social Justice Front." ESPN, May 24, 2018. http://www.espn.com/blog/nflnation/post/_/id/276029/why-the-nfl-is-light-years-behind-nba-on-social-justice-front

Katz, Celeste. 2018. "The WNBA Is Starting a New Season—of Activism—by Asking Fans to 'Take a Stand'." *Glamour*, May 17, 2018. https://www.glamour.com/story/wnba-take-a-seat-take-a-stand

Lee, Jane. 2018. "Maxwell to Stop Kneeling During Anthem." MLB.com, February 13, 2018. https://www.mlb.com/news/bruce-maxwell-to-stop-kneeling-in-protest/c-266388182

Nightengale, Bob. 2016. "Adam Jones on MLB's Lack of Kaepernick Protest: 'Baseball Is a White Man's Sport.'" *USA Today*, September 13, 2016. https://www.usatoday.com/story/sports/mlb/columnist/bob-nightengale/2016/09/12/adam-jones-orioles-colin-kaepernick-white-mans-sport/90260326/

Rapinoe, Megan. 2016. "Why I Am Kneeling." *The Players' Tribune*, October 16, 2016. https://www.theplayerstribune.com/en-us/articles/megan-rapinoe -why-i-am-kneeling

Schlager, Brandon. 2018. "Does the NHL Have a National Anthem Policy? Not Spe- cifically." *Sporting News*, May 23, 2018. http://www.sportingnews.com/us/ nhl/news/nhl-national-anthem-policy-rules-player-protests-union-nfl-colin -kaepernick/1mnlim80zk1511oh9mmzmzq40e

Seifert, Kevin. 2018. "How National Anthem Rules Differ across Sports Leagues." ESPN, May 24, 2018. http://www.espn.com/nfl/story/_/id/20848575/ rules-national-anthem-differ-sports-leagues

Taylor, Jon. 2017. "Bruce Maxwell Finally Broke MLB's Silence, and Hopefully Others Will Follow." *Sports Illustrated*, September 27, 2017. https:// www.si.com/mlb/2017/09/24/bruce-maxwell-anthem-protest

Debates on Patriotism and Constitutional Rights

Much of the debate surrounding the NFL player protests involves the appropriateness of the protests. Critics who consider them to be unpatriotic and disrespectful argue that players should not have the right to demonstrate during patriotic rituals reserved for the respectful appreciation of America and its ideals. In addition, many of these critics support the league's attempts to place restrictions on the players' ability to protest on the field.

For many supporters, however, exercising one of America's most impor- tant constitutional rights—the right to free speech—is part of America's fundamental values. In their opinion, the NFL players should not be deni- grated as ungrateful and unpatriotic; instead, they should be applauded for having the courage and fortitude to stand up to injustice despite strong condemnation—even from the president of the United States.

The Protests as Patriotic

As clearly articulated by both Colin Kaepernick and Eric Reid, the first NFL players to take a knee during the national anthem in September 2016, the pervasive mistreatment of people of color by U.S. law enforcement, as well as systematic racial injustice, motivated their protests. The demonstra- tions were an effort to raise awareness of these problems and inspire a movement for social change.

Throughout American history, the road to significant social change has always been rocky: inconvenient, dangerous, and even a threat to some seg- ments of the population. Crack downs from those in power on those who challenge the status quo is common.

"Look, I get the player protests are highly emotional issue," stated sports columnist Nancy Armour. "I also understand that some people will never be able to look beyond the method to hear the message. But protests aren't meant to make people comfortable—just the opposite, actually. To bring about change, people have to realize it's necessary. Democracy is hard, and it's often messy, but it's worth it. That's what's gotten lost here. Respecting the symbols of our freedom is pointless if we're not willing to respect and defend the ideals they represent" (Armour 2018).

The Protests as Unpatriotic

President Donald Trump is a vocal critic of the NFL player protests. On September 22, 2017, he condemned protesters during a rally in Alabama, calling the players unpatriotic and disrespectful. Moreover, he urged NFL owners to fire any player participating in the protests. His comments drew cheers from the crowd, further fueling the debate over American values and the meaning of patriotism.

Many NFL fans across the country agreed with the president. The more Trump called the protests anti-American and disrespectful to the nation's soldiers, the more fans came to believe it was true. A growing number of fans began to call for a league ban on the protests during the national anthem. NFL football, once regarded as a unifying sport enjoyed by all Americans, became divisive.

Critics of the protests maintained that players were largely to blame. "By long-standing tradition, liberals and conservatives alike show equal respect for flag-based rituals," observed conservative commentator Kyle Smith. "To disrespect the flag is understood to be a radical move, the kind of thing associated with the excesses of the Vietnam War movement. NFL players enjoy First Amendment rights to publicly shun or burn the flag if they so choose, but no corporation has a responsibility to tolerate the expression of such extreme ideas. Spurning the American Flag as a protest against the acts of some police officers is a radical stance that disgusts tens of millions of Americans" (Smith 2018).

Some critics assigned blame to the NFL, arguing that if the league had acted quickly and decisively against the protests they would not be in such a difficult situation. "The league allowed players and politicians alike to hijack the brand and turn it into a platform," maintained public relations executive David Fouse. "And while players are private citizens and certainly entitled to political expression, they are not entitled to take the brand of a private company and expose it to the criticism and censure of public leaders" (Fouse 2017).

The NFL's Policy Shift on the National Anthem

As the demonstrations continued throughout the 2017–2018 season, NFL team owners and league officials became increasingly concerned that the controversy over player protests during the national anthem were a major factor in flat TV ratings and attendance at games, which were affecting the bottom line. In order to ensure the financial well-being of the NFL, it became a priority to find a way to alleviate the controversy.

On May 23, 2018, NFL owners announced a new national anthem policy at the conclusion of their spring meetings. It required players and team personnel to stand if they were on the field during the anthem, but allowed an option for them to stay in the locker room. Teams whose players protest can be fined by the league.

NFL officials and team owners argued that the new policy was formulated to move past the controversy and put the focus back on football. Supporters of the policy regarded the change as in line with the patriotic image of the league and the conservative views of most NFL team owners. Many acknowledged the right of NFL players—and all Americans—to protest injustice but took issue with those protests occurring on the football field during a time-honored, patriotic ritual. They noted that although the U.S. Constitution protects free speech from government interference, private institutions can impose some limits on speech in the workplace.

Many on both sides of the political aisle defended players' rights to protest during the national anthem. Even many fans who didn't agree with the stated reasons for or the timing of the protests supported their right to protest, viewing it as a fundamental right.

"Fight for the rights of others that you would like to exercise yourself," conservative writer David French stated. "Do you want corporations obliterating speech the state can't touch? Do you want the price of participation in public debate to include the fear of lost livelihoods? Then, by all means, support the NFL.... Join the boycotts and shame campaigns. Watch this country's culture of liberty wither in front of our eyes" (French 2018).

Some critics pointed to an October 2017 Trump tweet threatening to take away tax breaks from the NFL because player protests supposedly constituted government interference. David Cole, American Civil Liberties Union (ACLU) national legal director, asserted, "The courts have recognized that when government officials threaten punishment or consequences because of protected speech, that in and of itself can chill the speech, in violation of the First Amendment" (quoted in Rosenberg 2018).

For many fans, the new NFL policy led to renewed appreciation of the patriotism inherent in the protests themselves. "Protest is patriotic," argued award-winning popular recording artist John Legend. "Protest has played a critically important role in elevating the voices of the most vulnerable in our nation. Protest in America has been essential in ending war, to demanding equal rights, to ending unfair practices that keep citizens marginalized. If we quell protest in the name of patriotism, we are not patriots. We are tyrants" (Legend 2017).

Further Reading

Armour, Nancy. 2018. "Trump Has No Right Questioning Patriotism of NFL Players." *USA Today*, July 20, 2018. https://www.usatoday.com/story/sports/col umnist/nancy-armour/2018/07/20/dont-distracted-trumps-latest-criticism -nfl-players/811007002/

Fouse, David. 2017. "The NFL Protests' Hidden Lesson: Don't Let Your Brand Get Hijacked by Politics." Fox News, October 17, 2017. http://www.foxnews .com/opinion/2017/10/23/nfl-protests-hidden-lesson-dont-let-your-brand -get-hijacked-by-politics.html

French, David. 2018. "Conservatives Fail the NFL's Free Speech Test." *New York Times*, May 24, 2018. https://www.nytimes.com/2018/05/24/opinion/ conservatives-fail-the-nfls-free-speech-test.html

Legend, John. 2017. "The NFL Protests Are Patriotic." *Slate*, September 24, 2017. http://www.slate.com/articles/news_and_politics/trials_and_error/2017/ 09/john_legend_on_why_the_nfl_protests_are_patriotic.html

Rosenberg, Eli. 2018. "What the NFL's New Rules for Anthem Protests Really Mean for the First Amendment, According to Experts." *Washington Post*, May 24, 2018. https://www.washingtonpost.com/news/early-lead/wp/2018/05/ 24/what-the-nfls-new-rules-for-anthem-protests-really-mean-for-the -first-amendment-according-to-experts/?noredirect=on&utm_term= .acb3698648f5

Smith, Kyle. 2018. "The NFL's Move against Anthem Protests Is Understandable." *National Review*, May 25, 2018. https://www.nationalreview.com/2018/05/ nfl-national-anthem-protest-move-understandable/

How People Perceive the National Anthem

A familiar symbol of American patriotism, the national anthem is meant to evoke patriotic feelings in all Americans. However, many people of color—Native Americans, African Americans, and other communities—see the anthem differently. For many African Americans, whose ancestors were oppressed under a slave system in 1814, the anthem is a product of a time when African Americans were oppressed and enslaved.

Race and the History of "The Star-Spangled Banner"

The national anthem's history began in conflict. Francis Scott Key, a wealthy lawyer, wrote a poem, "The Defence of Fort M'Henry," after witnessing the British bombardment of Fort McHenry near Baltimore, Maryland, in September 1814. Watching from a British ship eight miles away from the bombing, Key was inspired by the sight of the American flag surviving a brutal, all-night attack from British forces. Newspapers around the country printed Key's poem.

Most Americans are only familiar with the first stanza of "The Star-Spangled Banner"—the part that chronicles the brave defense of Fort McHenry. A third stanza, virtually forgotten today, refers to something more disturbing:

> Where is that band who so vauntingly swore,
> That the havoc of war and the battle's confusion
> A home and a Country should leave us no more?
> Their blood has wash'd out their foul footsteps pollution.
> No refuge could save the hireling and the slave
> From the terror of flight or the gloom of the grave,
> And the star-spangled banner in triumph doth wave
> O'er the land of the free and the home of the brave. (National Parks Service 2015)

It is widely believed that this third stanza refers to Key's hostility toward the Colonial Marines, a group of runaway slaves who fought alongside British forces and their hired mercenaries against the American side. In return, these slaves and their families received their freedom. Historians report that the black men in the Colonial Marines were a brave group. Key faced the Colonial Marines on August 24, 1814, at the Battle of Bladensburg. The battle did not go well for Key and his troops. In fact, after the British victory at Bladensburg, the Colonial Marines went on to take part in the burning of the White House, the Library of Congress, and the Capitol Building. In this stanza, Key appears to revel in the downfall of the black marines who fought against his men.

When Key's poem became the official national anthem of the United States in 1931, the published sheet music usually left out the controversial third stanza. This omission was not because of the reference to the slaves who had joined the British but rather because the stanza was considered insulting to the British, who by then had become American allies.

Protests as a Catalyst

After Colin Kaepernick and other league players began their protests, many people of color reexamined the very idea of patriotism, suggesting patriotism in the United States was never meant to include them. As Terrell Jermaine Starr asserted, "Patriotism has never been a racially equitable experience because it was never designed to be" (Starr 2017).

After Kaepernick's protests, this view caused people to take a critical look at the anthem's lyrics. The controversial third stanza of "The Star-Spangled Banner" was particularly disturbing. In the context of Key's hostility toward the Colonial Marines, critics read the third stanza as celebrating the deaths of freed black slaves fighting against him. "With Key still bitter that some black soldiers got the best of him a few weeks earlier," argued journalist Jason Johnson, " 'The Star-Spangled Banner' is as much a patriotic song as it is a diss track to black people who had the audacity to fight for their freedom" (Johnson 2016).

In light of charges that "The Star-Spangled Banner" was racist and written by a white American invested in a culture of white supremacy, many African Americans began to reexamine their own attitudes about the anthem and the concept of patriotism itself. "Like Kaepernick," social justice activist and journalist Shaun King concluded, "I've had enough of injustice in America and I've had enough of anthems written by bigots. Colin Kaepernick has provided a spark. 'The Star-Spangled Banner' should've never been made into our national anthem" (King 2016).

Calls to stop playing the national anthem before sporting events—or to replace "The Star-Spangled Banner" altogether—grew louder as many Americans questioned whether the song truly represented American ideals of equality.

Support for "The Star-Spangled Banner"

The NFL protests not only led Americans to take a closer look at the nation's patriotic symbols but also prompted Americans to defend them. To critics of the NFL demonstrations, player protests were disrespectful. They were offended when players refused to honor the patriotic ritual of standing at attention, facing the flag, and saluting by placing a hand over one's heart while listening to the anthem.

Some historians denied "The Star-Spangled Banner" is racist and fails to uphold American ideals. One key defense of Key and the national anthem comes from Mark Clague, a musicologist and professor of music history, who argues that the song's lyrics must be considered in the context of their time. He contends that the song celebrates the heroic effort of American forces to defend Fort McHenry, and that the American side, as well as the British side, included free and escaped black men. Clague argues Key held progressive views for his time on the issue of slavery: he freed several slaves that he had inherited from his family, he helped establish and run a school for freed children of color in Georgetown, and he founded the controversial American Colonization Society, which purchased slaves and transported them to freedom in Africa (Clague 2016).

Clague asserts the song is an appropriate national anthem because its words explore the nation's struggle to fulfill its promises of freedom and equality to all Americans. "After 'land of the free,' we have a question mark, not an exclamation point," he remarks. "Is the flag and what it represents still there? Are we winning the battle for freedom that this country was founded on? That's where Colin Kaepernick has started a productive conversation. If there are people who feel the song doesn't represent them, we need to pay attention to that. But if we just reject the song as racist, or declare that it isn't the anthem anymore, we don't fix the problem" (quoted in Schuessler 2016).

Further Reading

Clague, Mark. 2016. " 'Star-Spangled Banner' Critics Miss the Point." *CNN,* August 31, 2016. https://www.cnn.com/2016/08/31/opinions/star-spangled-banner-criticisms-opinion-clague/index.html

Johnson, Jason. 2016. "Star-Spangled Bigotry: The Hidden Racist History of the National Anthem." *The Root,* July 4, 2016. https://www.theroot.com/star-spangled-bigotry-the-hidden-racist-history-of-the-1790855893

King, Shaun. 2016. "King: Why I'll Never Stand Again for 'The Star-Spangled Banner'." *New York Daily News,* August 29, 2016. http://www.nydailynews.com/news/national/king-stand-star-spangled-banner-article-1.2770075#

National Parks Service. 2015. "The Star-Spangled Banner." Fort McHenry National Monument and Historic Shrine, Maryland. Last updated February 26, 2015. https://www.nps.gov/fomc/learn/historyculture/the-star-spangled-banner.htm

Schuesser, Jennifer. 2016. "Is the National Anthem Racist? Beyond the Debate over Colin Kaepernick." *New York Times,* September 2, 2016. https://www.nytimes.com/2016/09/03/arts/music/colin-kaepernick-national-anthem.html

Starr, Terrell Jermaine. 2017. "Patriotism Is for White People." *The Root,* September 25, 2017. https://www.theroot.com/patriotism-is-for-white-people-1818724099

NFL Protests and Race Relations

As the NFL player protests continued into the 2018 pro football season, the original reasons for the demonstrations were obscured by debates over free speech, NFL policy, respect for the flag and the military, and even the meaning of patriotism itself. At their core, however, the protests were always about racial inequality and mistreatment of people of color by the United States law enforcement and legal system. As journalist A. J. Willingham argues, "It [the protest] was about race, and all of the struggles that come with being a minority in America" (Willingham 2017).

To many, the national discussions surrounding the NFL player protests have been damaging to race relations in America, functioning to further divide an already polarized country. Others argue that these discussions are necessary in order to confront racially coded language and stereotypes.

The Origins of the Protest

Originally, the NFL protests were Colin Kaepernick's reaction to the killing of African American men during confrontations with white police officers. "I am not going to stand up to show pride in a flag for a country that oppresses black people and people of color," Kaepernick explained. "To me, this is bigger than football and it would be selfish on my part to look the other way. There are bodies on the street and people getting paid leave and getting away with murder" (Wyche 2016).

In order to keep the focus on the issues and to avoid being disrespectful to active military members and veterans, Kaepernick and his teammate Eric Reid consulted with Nate Boyer, an ex-Green Beret and former NFL player. The three men settled on player protesters taking a knee during the playing of the national anthem.

Divisive Rhetoric

By the start of the 2017–2018 season, the NFL protests caught the attention of President Donald Trump, who tweeted against them. Trump's supporters defended his attack, arguing that the national anthem wasn't the right time for protest and players had plenty of opportunities to protest social justice issues on their own time. Trump supporters announced fan boycotts of the NFL, which generated concern from NFL officials and owners when fan attendance and TV rating declined during the 2017–2018 season.

Many others, however, viewed Trump's comments as a racially coded attack. Calling black players obscene epithets and using the term *heritage*, a loaded word often associated with racist rhetoric, generated accusations that Trump used appeals to racism to enflame his supporters and further divide the American people along racial lines. Coming just a few weeks after Trump's initial refusal to condemn the deadly violence committed by alt-right activists, white supremacists, and neo-Nazi elements at a march in Charlottesville, Virginia, the president's attacks on NFL players appeared to be part of pattern to exploit racial tensions for partisan gain.

To critics of the protest, however, the protesters themselves were the ones inflaming racial tensions and hatred toward law enforcement. Critics argued that instead of taking a knee, players should use their popularity to challenge racial stereotypes and biases off the playing field, not on it. "The bottom line is that sports stars would do well to get off their knees and lead a constructive conversation on race," commentator Brian Dean Wright wrote. "If they can't do that, maybe they should just stick to playing sports" (Wright 2017).

Public Opinion

Public opinion polls confirmed this division over the NFL player protests. According to a 2018 HuffPost/YouGov poll, 49 percent of Americans said it was inappropriate for players to kneel during the anthem, while 35 percent said it was appropriate (Edwards-Levy 2018). Along racial lines, 60 percent of white Americans believed it was inappropriate, compared to 60 percent of black Americans who thought it was appropriate to kneel in protest during the anthem (Edwards-Levy 2018).

This racial division over the NFL protests was part of a larger perception that race relations in the United States were deteriorating under the Trump administration, especially given Trump's controversial comments after the violent alt-right march in Charlottesville. According to an August 2018 CBS/YouGov poll, 61 percent of respondents believed racial tensions had increased in the year since Charlottesville (Salvanto 2018).

The poll also found that 58 percent of Americans disapproved of Trump's handling of racial issues, while 41 percent approved. Broken down along partisan lines, 83 percent of Republicans approved of Trump's handling of racial issues, while 90 percent of Democrats disapproved. When asked about Trump's criticism of athletes, 65 percent of Republicans approved, while only 32 percent of all Americans approved (Salvanto 2018).

In light of public opinion on race relations in the United States and Trump's handling of the issue, political analysts maintained that Trump used the NFL protests to appeal to his Republican base, which was largely white and older, at the expense of Democratic voters, who tend to be younger and more diverse.

The New NFL National Anthem Policy

Whether athletes should protest and in what ways it was acceptable for them to protest became an issue after the NFL passed a controversial new national anthem policy in spring 2018. The new policy required players and team personnel to stand if they were on the field during the anthem; however, they had the option to stay in the locker room. Violation of the policy could result in league fines.

Supporters of the new policy argued that it would take the controversy off of the table and allow teams to focus on the game. Football could once again be a unifier in American society, not a divider. Athletes would still have opportunities for self-expression—just not during the national anthem.

To critics, the new policy represented an attempt by NFL ownership to stifle the freedom of speech of black players in order to satisfy critics of the protests. Issues of racial inequality and police brutality, the actual reason for the NFL player protests, were downplayed while concerns over falling TV ratings and critical presidential tweets took priority.

Some accused the NFL of having a plantation mentality, a term referring to the plantation system of the Deep South during slavery. "[That] 30 team owners all of them wealthy and privileged, most of them white and Republican approved this policy limiting the free expression of a mostly black male work force is proof of just how tone deaf and prone to plantation mentality the NFL is" (*Sacramento Bee* 2018).

As outrage over the new NFL policy increased, a growing number of African American fans considered boycotting the league. Karen Attiah, an African American editor and reporter, asserted, "Black fans can take a stand against the league by refusing to watch the games or buy merchandise or game tickets. Why should we support an organization that wants to silence us? This is about way more than football. For many of us black people, this is our lives. None of this is a game" (Attiah 2018).

The 2018–2019 NFL Season

Just a few weeks before the first preseason games of the 2018–2019 season, the NFL announced it would delay implementing its new national anthem policy. When the 2018 NFL preseason launched, player protests during the national anthem resumed. On Twitter, President Trump renewed his aggressive criticism of the protesters.

Critics called Trump's condemnation another cynical political ploy. "At a time when the president faces a range of political and legal controversies—not the least the ongoing Russia probe implicating him, his family and close associates—the new NFL season brings Trump an opportunity to heighten attention on his ongoing feud with the African American players, a wedge issue that animates a number of his white voters heading into the November [2018] midterm elections" (Stokols 2018).

As the one-year anniversary of the tragic events in Charlottesville approached, many people argued that Trump should not be tweeting about NFL player protests, which only stoked racial tensions. Instead, they said, he should work to heal the nation's racial divisions.

Further Reading

"The Anthem/Balls and Strikes/Magic Man." 2016. *Real Sports with Bryant Gumbel*, season 22, episode 9, produced by Tim Walker (segment), starring Bryant Gumbel, aired on September 27, 2016, on HBO.

Attiah, Karen. 2018. "It's Time to Cancel the NFL and Its Plantation-Style Politics." *Washington Post*, May 24, 2018. https://www.washingtonpost.com/blogs/post-partisan/wp/2018/05/24/its-time-to-cancel-the-nfl-and-its-plantation-style-politics/?utm_term=.710e69141faf

Edwards-Levy, Ariel. 2018. "Americans Are Split Over the NFL's Decision on Anthem Protests." *Huffington Post*, May 29, 2018. https://www.huffingtonpost.com/entry/americans-split-over-nfl-anthem-protest-ruling_us_5b0dc5ade4b0568a880f7e9b

Sacramento Bee Editorial Board. 2018. "'Stand and Show Respect' for the National Anthem? That's the NFL's Plantation Mentality." *Sacramento Bee*, May 23, 2018. https://www.sacbee.com/opinion/editorials/article211766199.html

Salvanto, Anthony. 2018. "Poll: One Year after Charlottesville, Majority of Americans See Racial Tensions on the Rise." *CBS News*, August 12, 2018. https://www.cbsnews.com/news/poll-one-year-after-charlottesville-americans-see-racial-tensions-on-increase/

Stokols, Eli. 2018. "New Season, Same Trump: The President Again Blasts NFL Players for Protests during National Anthem." *Los Angeles Times*, August 10, 2018. http://www.latimes.com/politics/la-na-pol-trump-nfl-20180810-story.html

Tatum, Sophie. 2017. "Trump: NFL Owners Should Fire Players Who Protest the National Anthem." CNN, September 23, 2017. https://www.cnn.com/2017/09/22/politics/donald-trump-alabama-nfl/index.html

Trump, Donald (@realDonaldTrump). 2018. *Twitter.com,* August 10, 2018. https://
      twitter.com/realDonaldTrump/status/1027892043908046849

Willingham, A. J. 2017. "The #TakeAKnee Protests Have Always Been about Race.
      Period." CNN, September 27, 2017. https://www.cnn.com/2017/09/27/us/
      nfl-anthem-protest-race-trump-trnd/index.html

Wright, Bryan Dean. 2017. "NFL Protests: Stars Should Get off Their Knees and
      Lead a Constructive Conversation on Race." Fox News, September 25,
      2017. http://www.foxnews.com/opinion/2017/09/25/nfl-protests-stars
      -should-get-off-their-knees-and-lead-constructive-conversation-on
      -race.html

Wyche, Steve. 2016. "Colin Kaepernick Explains Why He Sat during National
      Anthem." NFL.com, August 28, 2016. http://www.nfl.com/news/story/
      0ap3000000691077/article/colin-kaepernick-explains-protest-of-national
      -anthem

Issues of Racial Inequality and Police Brutality

The NFL player protests have always been against racial inequality and
police brutality. But critics, including President Donald Trump, have deliberately distracted attention from the reasons for the demonstrations and
have focused instead on debates about patriotism, the flag and the anthem,
and support for the military. Despite these efforts to hijack the protests, the
national debate they generated has managed to raise awareness about systematic racial inequality in America, particularly the way law enforcement
and the criminal justice system discriminate against people of color.

The Origins of the NFL Player Protests

Just weeks before the NFL national anthem protests began in
August 2016, two police officers shot Alton Sterling, a young black man,
at close range outside a convenience store in Baton Rouge, Louisiana. The
two officers involved claimed Sterling was reaching for a gun hidden in
the waistband of his pants. A bystander's video of the incident shocked
viewers and sparked calls for justice.

Colin Kaepernick, star quarterback for the San Francisco 49ers, was one
of many Americans outraged by Sterling's death. "This is what lynchings
look like in 2016!" he posted on Instagram. "Another murder in the streets
because the color of a man's skin, at the hands of people who say they will
protect us" (@Kaepernick7 July 6, 2016).

During the national anthem before the first few preseason games, Kaepernick sat on the bench instead of standing alongside his teammates.
When asked about it, Kaepernick characterized his decision as a reaction

to the racial discrimination faced by blacks in American society, particularly the epidemic of police brutality disproportionately affecting the African American community.

After the third preseason game, Kaepernick's teammate Eric Reid asked him how he could help bring attention to matters that concerned both players. "We spoke at length about many of the issues that face our community, including systematic oppression of people of color, police brutality, and the criminal justice system," recalled Reid. "We also discussed how we could use our platform, provided to us by being professional athletes in the N.F.L., to speak for those who are voiceless" (Reid 2017).

On September 1, 2016, Reid joined Kaepernick in taking a knee during the national anthem. Other NFL players would do the same in the ensuing weeks of the 2016–2017 season.

Racial Inequality and Police Brutality

As writer Megan Garber observed, the reasons for the NFL national anthem protests were clearly articulated by the men who participated in them. "The players are not, as a whole, protesting the national anthem. . . . They are not protesting the flag. They are protesting police brutality against African Americans. They are protesting the lack of legal accountability for the officers who enact that violence. They are protesting, more broadly, the ways racism gets codified in America, the ways it is expanded from a personal evil into a societal one" (Garber 2017).

A 2015 study in *The Guardian* found that young black men were nine times more likely than other Americans to be killed by police officers despite making up only 2 percent of the U.S. population (Swaine, Laughland, Larty, and McCarthy 2015). According to researchers, about one in every 65 deaths of a young African American man in the United States is at the hands of police (Swaine, Laughland, Larty, and McCarthy, 2015). A 2018 study, however, disputed the theory that minorities are disproportionately killed by police officers. It found that less than one percent of victims of police killing were unarmed (Menifield, Shin, and Strother 2018).

A series of high-profile police-involved killings of African American men brought attention to the issue. On July 17, 2014, Eric Garner died after a New York City police officer held him in a chokehold after a confrontation over selling individual cigarettes. Less than a month later, a white police officer, Darren Wilson, shot and killed an unarmed Michael Brown in Ferguson, Missouri, which led to protests and violence. In October of that year, a white police officer shot Laquan McDonald 16 times while the black teenager was walking away from a police car in Chicago. A white police officer also killed 12-year-old Tamir Rice for holding a replica gun in Cleveland, Ohio, later that year. On July 16, 2017, police shot into a car and killed Philando Castile, outside of St. Paul, Minnesota, an incident live-streamed on Facebook by his girlfriend, who was also in the car. Alton Sterling's killing occurred just a few weeks later.

Kaepernick's protests began a month after Sterling's death. "I am not going to stand up to show pride in a flag for a country that oppresses black people and people of color," he explained. "To me, this is bigger than football and it would be selfish on my part to look the other way. There are bodies on the street and people getting paid leave and getting away with murder" (Wyche 2016).

The Backlash

Even as NFL players clearly identified the reasons for the player protests, critics tried to shift the focus to issues of the flag and the anthem, the military, and national pride. Critics derided protesters for what they said was disrespectful and unpatriotic behavior during the anthem. Some fans supported the players' right to voice their opinion on social justice problems in the United States, but opposed their choice of protesting on the job during patriotic rituals. President Trump, as well as others, questioned their knowledge of the issues involved and argued that their wealth and privileged position complicated their message.

As criticism of the protests mounted and the NFL initiated discussions on a new NFL policy, players expressed frustration that critics were distracting from the real reason for the demonstrations. "It baffles me that our protest is still being misconstrued as disrespectful to the country, flag, and military personnel," Reid wrote. "We chose it because it is exactly the opposite. It has always been my understanding that the brave men and women who fought and died for our country did so to ensure that we could live in a fair and free society, which includes the right to speak out in protest" (Reid 2017).

To Kneel or Not to Kneel

In July 2018, after the new NFL policy on protests and the anthem was delayed, debates over the future of the protests continued.

Many fans believed the protests were ineffective because of the controversy. "I want the players to fight for their right to speak out, but I also want them to put their spotlight back on police violence," writer Touré argued. "When players kneel during the anthem, it shows they have a Black political consciousness that they're willing to share in a dignified way. I have maximum respect for those who have kneeled, but it may be time for players to find a new way to express themselves on this issue in order to put the focus back on police violence" (Touré 2018).

Others, however, believed the protests should continue, even if only a few NFL players participated every week. One supporter was basketball legend and social justice activist Kareem Abdul-Jabbar. "All progressive movements met with strong resistance at first, but constant protest leads to reform," he said. "We already know that many were not keen to abandon slavery. Nor were many anxious to give women the vote, eliminate child labor, abolish Jim Crow laws, end the Vietnam War. These reforms were accomplished over time by protesters who held their ground despite lack of popularity. History has honored them as admired patriots. As long as there are players, no matter how few, out there every week showing their courage in the face of other's timidity, the protests are effective" (Abdul-Jabbar 2018).

Further Reading

Abdul-Jabbar, Kareem. 2018. "Why the NFL Player Protests Still Matter." *The Guardian,* February 3, 2018. https://www.theguardian.com/sport/2018/feb/03/why-the-nfl-player-protests-still-matter

Garber, Megan. 2017. "They Took a Knee." *The Atlantic,* September 24, 2017. https://www.theatlantic.com/entertainment/archive/2017/09/why-the-nfl-is-protesting/540927/

Kaepernick, Colin (@*Kaepernick7*). 2016. Instagram photo, July 6, 2016. https://www.instagram.com/p/BHhetl8g_EE/

Menifield, Charles E., Geiguen Shin, and Logan Strother. 2018. "Do White Law Enforcement Officers Target Minority Suspects?" *Public Administration Review,* June 19, 2018. https://onlinelibrary.wiley.com/doi/abs/10.1111/puar.12956

Reid, Eric. 2017. "Eric Reid: Why Colin Kaepernick and I Decided to Take a Knee." *New York Times,* September 23, 2017. https://www.nytimes.com/2017/09/25/opinion/colin-kaepernick-football-protests.html

Schad, Tom. 2018. "Donald Trump Says He Doesn't Believe NFL Players Who Protest during Anthem Have a 'Real Issue'." *USA Today,* June 15, 2018. https://www.usatoday.com/story/sports/nfl/2018/06/15/donald-trump-nfl-national-anthem-protest-players-no-issue/704930002/

Swaine, Jon, Oliver Laughland, Jamiles Lartey, and Ciara McCarthy. 2015. "Young Black Men Killed by Police at Highest Rate in Year of 1,134 Deaths." *The Guardian,* December 31, 2015. https://www.theguardian.com/us-news/2015/dec/31/the-counted-police-killings-2015-young-black-men

Touré. 2018. "The NFL and White America Have Polluted #TakeAKnee So Much That Maybe Players Should Find New Ways to Protest." *The Grio*, May 25, 2018. https://thegrio.com/2018/05/25/the-nfl-white-america -killed-takeaknee-players-find-new-ways-to-protest/

Trump, Donald (@realDonaldTrump). 2018. Twitter, August 10, 2018. https:// twitter.com/realDonaldTrump/status/1027892043908046849

Wyche, Steve. 2016. "Colin Kaepernick Explains Why He Sat during National Anthem." NFL.com, August 28, 2016. http://www.nfl.com/news/story/ 0ap3000000691077/article/colin-kaepernick-explains-protest-of-national -anthem

The NFL's Image and Popularity

The sport of baseball is known as America's pastime. Professional football, however, is the most popular of U.S. spectator sports. NFL football surged past baseball to became America's favorite sport in the mid-1960s— and has remained in the top spot ever since. In fact, a 2018 Gallup poll found that 37 percent of American adults identified NFL football as their favorite spectator sport (Norman 2018).

As professional football surged in popularity during the 1960s, the NFL implemented a strategy to brand itself as the most patriotic professional sports league in the United States. This conservative, all-American image appealed to many Americans. However, it made the league particularly susceptible to divisive attacks and questions over the true nature of patriotism when NFL players began protesting racial inequality and police brutality during the 2016 NFL season.

NFL Brand Strategy

Since the NFL was established in 1922, it has competed against other popular American sports to attract fan attention. In the early twentieth century, the main rival of professional football was college football, which benefited from loyal alumni fan bases and traditional regional rivalries. Before long, however, professional football developed its own rivalries and fan bases, increasing its popularity. Another boon to the NFL's status was a series of rule changes that made the game faster and higher scoring. League expansion resulted in larger fan bases, and the national broadcast of games by the late 1950s allowed NFL teams to challenge the dominance of major league baseball for the hearts of American sports fans.

During the mid-1960s, America's involvement in the Vietnam War (1955–1975) increased. A military draft called increasing numbers of young

American men for duty. During World War II (1939–1945), 638 NFL players were called up and served in the military (Berrett 2017). In contrast, during the Vietnam War many draft-eligible athletes were protected from being called for active duty by league officials and team owners. Instead, they were placed with the National Guard and reserve units, despite long waiting lists. According to historian Jesse Berrett, only six NFL players served in the Vietnam War (Berrett 2017). At that time, public opinion polls showed that many Americans resented this preferential treatment of professional athletes when it came to military service.

To counter the image of NFL players as a group of coddled sports celebrities unwilling to sacrifice for the war effort, the league began to incorporate more patriotic symbols and pageantry into its broadcasts. The NFL commissioner at the time, Pete Rozelle, described the marketing strategy as "a conscious effort on our part to bring the element of patriotism into the Super Bowl" (Berrett 2017). That meant that an increasing number of NFL games featured Air Force flyovers, rousing patriotic music, flag imagery, and ceremonies to honor war heroes and fallen soldiers.

According to Berrett, "The NFL's intention was to persuade audiences both popular and elite that the sport deserved support because it was quintessentially American, perfectly in tune with the contemporary world, and deserving of solicitude should it encounter any legal roadblocks" (Berrett 2018).

By the 1970s, the NFL strategy to market itself as the essential American sport had paid off. Politicians from both sides of the aisle solicited political and financial support from NFL owners and players, who found financial advantages in cultivating those connections. As it cemented its position as the most popular sport in America, NFL football was also inextricably tying itself to the military, the U.S. political establishment, and conservative symbols of patriotism like the flag and the national anthem.

The Paid Patriotism Controversy

The NFL's long-standing strategy of promoting a brand of patriotism that links love of country with love of the military proved to be a good financial strategy. A shady side of this connection between football and the military was revealed in 2015, when a joint oversight report released by Arizona Republican senators Jeff Flake and John McCain detailed the results of an investigation into payments made by the Department of Defense (DoD) to professional sports leagues, including the NFL, Major League Baseball, the National Basketball Association, and the National Hockey League.

According to the investigation, the DoD paid more than $6.8 million to professional sports leagues between 2012 and 2015 to hold events honoring the U.S. military, including "on-field color guard performances, enlistment and re-enlistment ceremonies, performances of the national anthem, full-field flag details, and ceremonial first pitch and puck drops" (Flake and McCain 2015).

The majority of those payments—$6 million—went to the NFL. The Atlanta Falcons received the highest amount of money to allow patriotic displays, acquiring $879,000 from the DoD.

Known as the paid patriotism controversy, the scandal received widespread criticism from public officials, sport commentators, and fans, which prompted a quick end to the practice. The NFL's promotion of the military was exposed as mainly a cynical marketing ploy and just another source of revenue for wealthy team owners. The controversy injected a note of uncertainty regarding which patriotic displays were authentic and which were manipulative marketing efforts to attract more viewership. As the senators' report maintained, "Unsuspecting audience members became the subjects of paid-marketing campaigns, rather than simply bearing witness to teams' authentic, voluntary shows of support for the brave men and women who wear our nation's uniform" (Flake and McCain 2015).

The NFL National Anthem Protests

When NFL players began protesting racial injustice and police brutality by kneeling during the national anthem in 2016, many owners and league officials immediately saw the threat to the NFL brand. Roger Goodell, the current NFL commissioner, recognized how the controversy could damage the league's financial survival. "We live in a country that can feel very divided," he noted in a memo to league and team officials. "Sports, and especially the NFL, bring people together and lets them set aside those divisions, at least for a few hours. The current dispute over the National Anthem is threatening to erode the unifying power of our game, and is now dividing us, and our players, from many fans across the country" (Baker 2017).

Goodell's concerns were well founded. As the protests continued through the 2017 season, NFL TV ratings and game attendance declined. According to experts, the NFL's 2017 regular-season TV ratings were down almost 9 percent over the year before (Deitsch 2018). Moreover, although 37 percent of Americans identified pro football as their favorite sport to watch in 2017, that figure was down from 43 percent in 2006 and 2007.

This drop in TV viewing and game attendance seemed to occur for many reasons, some unrelated to the protests. Some people attributed it to fewer people watching television overall and too many football games on television. The league's apparent mishandling of chronic head injuries was another reason for the sport's decline in popularity, as many fans came to believe that owners and league officials placed financial issues over the well-being of the players.

During the 2017 season, however, the perception that the NFL protests were the central cause of the NFL's growing image problems and declining popularity came to dominate the national discussion about pro football. According to a September 2017 Morning Consult poll, 44 percent of respondents said that the player demonstrations led them to view the NFL less favorably, a view split along age and racial lines (Easley 2017).

The more Trump reframed the player protests as anti-American and disrespectful to the nation's soldiers, the more fans came to believe it was true and that the protests should be banned. Once a unifying and patriotic brand, the NFL was now the most polarizing professional sports league in the United States.

"While NFL officials often argue that football is apolitical," journalist P. R. Lockhart wrote, "it was the prominence of the sport and the league's ongoing efforts to tie itself to patriotism in the American consciousness that made it easy for President Trump to wield patriotism as a way of dismissing those involved in the kneeling protest. In doing so, Trump managed to change the subject by casting protesting NFL players—the majority of whom are black; all of whom were drawing explicit attention to racial inequality—as a danger to the ideals of America" (Lockhart 2018).

The League Makes a Move

On May 23, 2018, NFL owners announced a new national anthem policy at the conclusion of their spring meetings. Although the new policy satisfied many Americans who had come to believe that the player protests had to be shut down, it also generated criticism from many others who supported the players' right to demonstrate for social justice issues. Unlike the National Basketball Association, a professional sports league that was careful to keep player activism separate from the game itself and yet continued to support its players' right to free speech, the NFL doubled down on its conservative image and implemented restrictions on the free speech of its players.

Steve Kerr, the head coach of the NBA's Golden State Warriors, pointed out the difference between the brand image of the NFL and the NBA. "I think it's just typical of the NFL," he stated. "They're just trying to play to their fan base and basically trying to use the anthem as fake patriotism, nationalism, scaring people. It's idiotic, but that's how the NFL has handled their business. I'm proud to be in a league that understands that patriotism in America is about free speech and about peaceful protesting" (Beer 2018).

The NFL's Image Going Forward

After the NFL paused its new policy on the national anthem protests when it came under fire, the league announced the policy would be reassessed. For many, the enduring controversy over the policy revealed the league's lack of options on the issue and the serious damage done to the NFL brand.

"The NFL has now backed itself into a corner: Trump will continue to fan the flames, players are rightfully infuriated, and the need for the protest itself feels more acute than ever," journalist Claire McNear observed. "It's hard to imagine that the league failed to foresee any of this, so we're left with one explanation: The league chose branded patriotism above its players and above its communities—and maybe now even above itself" (McNear 2018).

Further Reading

Baker, Geoff. 2017. "National Anthem Controversy Hurting the NFL's Brand." *Seattle Times,* October 15, 2017. https://www.seattletimes.com/sports/sea hawks/national-anthem-controversy-hurting-the-nfls-brand/

Beer, Jeff. 2018. "The NBA and NFL Offer Opposite Versions of American Brand Image." *Fast Company,* May 25, 2018. https://www.fastcompany.com /40577903/the-nba-and-nfl-offer-opposite-versions-of-american-brand -image

Berrett, Jesse. 2017. "The NFL Marketing Ploy That Was Too Successful for the League's Own Good." *Washington Post,* December 10, 2017. https:// www.washingtonpost.com/news/made-by-history/wp/2017/12/10/the-nfl -marketing-ploy-that-was-too-successful-for-the-leagues-own-good/?utm _term=.76a7da94cb38

Berrett, Jesse. 2018. "How the NFL and American Politicians Politicized (and Helped Merchandise) Pro Football." Whatitmeanstobeamerican.org, July 5, 2018. http://www.whatitmeanstobeamerican.org/identities/how-the-nfl -and-american-politicians-politicized-and-helped-merchandise-pro-football/

Deitsch, Richard. 2018. "Why the NFL's Ratings Saw a Steep Decline in 2017." *Sports Illustrated,* January 3, 2018. https://www.si.com/tech-media/2018/ 01/03/nfl-ratings-decline-espn-fox-nbc-network-tv

Easley, Cameron. 2017. "Poll: Anthem Protests Dent Views of NFL, but Not among All U.S. Adults." *Morning Consult,* October 4, 2017. https://morningconsult.com /2017/10/04/anthem-protests-take-toll-on-nfl-popularity/

Flake, Jeff, and John McCain. 2015. *Tackling Paid Patriotism: A Joint Oversight Report,* 2015. https://www.mccain.senate.gov/public/_cache/files/ 12de6dcb-d8d8-4a58-8795-562297f948c1/tackling-paid-patriotism -oversight-report.pdf

Lockhart, P. R. 2018. "Trump's Reaction to the NFL Protests Shows How He Fights the Culture War." *Vox,* February 4, 2018. https://www.vox.com/identities/2018/2/4/16967902/nfl-protests-patriotism-race-donald-trump-super-bowl

McNear, Claire. 2018. "Why Is the NFL So Obsessed with Patriotism?" *The Ringer,* May 24, 2018. https://www.theringer.com/nfl/2018/5/24/17390164/national-anthem-football-owners-donald-trump-patriotism-politics

Norman, Jim. 2018. "Football Still Americans' Favorite Sport to Watch." *Gallup,* January 4, 2018. https://news.gallup.com/poll/224864/football-americans-favorite-sport-watch.aspx

CHAPTER FOUR

Profiles

This section provides biographical profiles of important figures in the recent wave of NFL player protests, including Colin Kaepernick, Eric Reid, military veteran and former NFL player Nate Boyer, Donald Trump, and NFL executives.

Boyer, Nate (1981–)

Former NFL player and military veteran who inspired Colin Kaepernick to kneel in protest

Nate Boyer was born on January 9, 1981, in Oak Ridge, Tennessee. He grew up in El Cerrito, California. After graduating from high school, he moved to Los Angeles to become an actor. In 2004, he traveled to Sudan as an aid worker to help refugees of the genocide that ravaged the Darfur region of the country. Upon his return to the United States, he joined the U.S. Army, becoming a Green Beret in 2006. Over the next six years, he served multiple tours in Iraq and Afghanistan during Operation Enduring Freedom.

After his military service ended, Boyer enrolled at the University of Texas, where he earned a spot on the football team despite a lack of football experience. During his college football career, he earned several awards for academic excellence. In 2012 he received the Disney Spirit Award, which is given to the most inspirational figure in college football. He was also the first recipient of the Armed Forces Merit Award given by the Football Writers Association of America.

The Seattle Seahawks signed Boyer as a free agent in 2015. In a preseason game against the Denver Broncos, he participated in three plays, recording one tackle. A few days later, the team released him.

During the first few preseason games of the 2016 season, Colin Kaepernick, the quarterback of the San Francisco 49ers, protested social and racial injustice and police brutality against African Americans by sitting on the sidelines during the national anthem. Boyer responded by writing an open letter to Kaepernick, published in the *Army Times* on August 30. In it, Boyer conveyed his admiration for Kaepernick's courage and idealism but told him the idea of a player sitting on the bench during the national anthem implied a disrespect for the sacrifices active soldiers and military veterans have made to protect the country over the years.

Boyer closed the letter with a vow to keep listening. "Even though my initial reaction to your protest was one of anger, I'm trying to listen to what you're saying and why you're doing it," he stated. "When I told my mom about this article, she cautioned me that 'the last thing our country needed right now was more hate.' As usual, she's right. There are already plenty people fighting fire with fire, and it's just not helping anyone or anything. So I'm just going to keep listening, with an open mind" (Boyer 2016).

Kaepernick read Boyer's letter and the two men met to discuss Boyer's concerns about the protest. The goal was to find a way for Kaepernick to protest without dishonoring those who have served the country. "We sorta came to a middle ground where he would take a knee alongside his teammates," Boyer recalled in an episode of *Real Sports*. "Soldiers take a knee in front of a fallen brother's grave, you know, to show respect. When we're on a patrol, you know, and we go into a security halt, we take a knee and pull a security" (*Real Sports* 2016).

Kaepernick liked the suggestion. "He said, 'I think that would be—I think—I think that would be very powerful,'" Boyer recounted. "And, you know, he asked me to do it with him. And I said, 'Look, I'll stand next to you. I gotta stand though. I gotta stand with my hand on my heart. That's just—that's just what I do and where I'm from'" (*Real Sports* 2016). On September 1, Kaepernick took a knee during the national anthem. His teammate, Eric Reid, joined him. Boyer stood next to Kaepernick on the sidelines, his hand over his heart.

Kaepernick later explained that the meeting with Boyer was the reason for the change in tactics. "We [Kaepernick and Reid] were talking to him about how can we get the message back on track and not take away from the military, not take away from fighting for our country, but keep the focus on what the issues are," he explained. "And as we talked about it, we came up with taking a knee. Because there are issues that still need to be addressed and it was also a way to show respect to the men and women who fight for this country" (Thomas 2016).

Although Boyer, Kaepernick, and Reid received support from many quarters for the change in tactics, other fans, sports journalists, and political commentators continued to call the protests inappropriate and unpatriotic. Moreover, many veterans criticized Boyer for getting involved in the first place with such a controversial issue.

For Boyer, the goal was to keep moving forward to inspire positive social change. "So now that you have everyone's attention, what are you going to do with that?" he recalled asking Kaepernick. "How are you going to take action? That's the key right now. A lot of people want to know what you're going to do about it. If you're going to bring attention to a situation, you not only have to devise a plan, but you have to have measurables of what you want to achieve, what you're looking for and what for you, in the simplest form, what will get you back up on your feet for the anthem? What do you need to see?" (Wagoner 2016).

By 2017, however, Boyer had come to the realization that divisiveness and partisanship was in danger of tearing the country apart. "Simply put, it seems like we just hate each other; and that is far more painful to me than any protest, or demonstration, or rally, or tweet," he observed in an open letter to the American people. "We're told to pick a side, there's a line drawn in the sand, 'are you with us or against us?' It's just not who we are, or at least who we're supposed to be; we're supposed to be better than that, we're Americans. This doesn't even seem to be about right or wrong anymore, but more about right or left" (Boyer 2017).

Boyer closes the letter with a call for greater understanding and national unity. "So please, no more lines in the sand, not at home, not among our people. No more choosing sides, no more 'for or against.' I believe our Veterans will be called upon to lead the way in healing the world and solving its problems; right now our country needs that more than I can remember. . . . Let's get this thing fixed together, you and me" (Boyer 2017).

Further Reading

"The Anthem/Balls and Strikes/Magic Man." 2016. *Real Sports with Bryant Gumbel*, season 22, episode 9, produced by Tim Walker (segment), starring Bryant Gumbel, aired on September 27, 2016, on HBO.

Boyer, Nate. 2016. "An Open Letter to Colin Kaepernick, from a Green Beret-Turned-Long Snapper." *Army Times*, August 30, 2016. https://www.armytimes.com/opinion/2016/08/30/an-open-letter-to-colin-kaepernick-from-a-green-beret-turned-long-snapper/

Boyer, Nate. 2017. "Ex-Green Beret Nate Boyer Writes Open Letter to Kaepernick, Trump, NFL, and America." ESPN, October 13, 2017. http://www .espn.com/nfl/story/_/id/21003968/nfl-2017-ex-green-beret-nate-boyer -writes-open-letter-president-donald-trump-colin-kaepernick-nfl-united -states-america

Thomas, Jenna. 2016. "Colin Kaepernick Joined by 49ers Teammate Eric Reid in National Anthem Protest." *SBNation* (blog), September 2, 2016. https:// www.sbnation.com/2016/9/1/12761798/colin-kaepernick-joined-by-eric -reid-national-anthem-protest-niners-chargers

Wagoner, Nick. 2016. "From a Seat to a Knee: How Colin Kaepernick and Nate Boyer Are Trying to Effect Change." ESPN, September 6, 2016. http:// www.espn.com/blog/san-francisco-49ers/post/_/id/19253/from-a-seat-to -a-knee-how-colin-kaepernick-and-nate-boyer-are-trying-to-affect-change

Goodell, Roger (1959–)

NFL Commissioner since 2006

On February 15, 1959, Roger Goodell was born in Jamestown, New York. His family moved to Bronxville, a suburb of New York City, when he was a young man. As a student at Washington and Jefferson College, Goodell played on the football team, but a serious knee injury ended his football career during his freshman season. In 1981, he graduated from college with a degree in economics.

Goodell wrote letters to every NFL team to enquire about entry-level job opportunities. His efforts paid off. In 1982, he was hired as an intern in the NFL offices in New York City, where he worked with top league officials. A year later, he took a job as an intern for the New York Jets and by 1984 returned to the league office in the public relations department. Over the next couple of decades, Goodell advanced through the ranks, becoming director of international development and club administration in 1990 and chief operating officer in 2001. In 2006, he was chosen to be the next NFL commissioner.

As commissioner, Goodell has generated controversy over his management of a number of serious and complicated issues. For example, he drew criticism for his slow response to the rising number of chronic traumatic encephalopathy diagnoses in former football players. He also was criticized for his handling of several scandals involving players and coaches. He announced a new NFL Personal Conduct Policy, which imposed stronger penalties on players accused of violations such as domestic abuse, drunk driving, the use of banned substances, and other issues both on and off the field. Although the new policy was welcomed, Goodell was criticized for taking so long to get tough on offenders. Goodell also faced fire from fans and media over his role in labor negotiations with players and game officials: in 2011, stalled negotiations led to a five-month lockout of NFL players, while replacement referees were used for a few weeks during a 2012 lockout of game officials.

At the beginning of the 2016 preseason, Goodell faced one of the biggest public relations crises of his career when Colin Kaepernick began his protests. Within a few weeks, Kaepernick's bench sitting evolved to kneeling, and other players around the league took part in similar actions.

Goodell expressed support for Kaepernick's activism on social justice issues, but he opposed Kaepernick's his methods. "I support our players when they want to see change in society, and we don't live in a perfect society," Goodell stated. "We live in an imperfect society. On the other hand, we believe very strongly in patriotism in the NFL. I personally believe very strongly in that. I think it's important to have respect for our country, for our flag, for the people who make our country better; for law enforcement, and for our military who are out fighting for our freedoms and our ideals" (NFL.com 2016).

For Goodell, the role of football is to unite the country, not divide it. "We encourage our players to be respectful in that time and I like to think of it as a moment where we can unite as a country," he asserted. "And that's what we need more, and that's what I think football does—it unites our country. So I would like to see us focusing on our similarities and trying to bring people together" (NFL.com 2016).

In the following weeks, Goodell began to work with a group of players on social justice issues, including criminal justice reform and improving community relations between law enforcement and community members.

On September 22, 2017, however, President Donald Trump escalated the controversy when he blasted the protesters during a rally in Alabama, calling the players unpatriotic and disrespectful. He also recommended that the NFL owners fire any player participating in the protests.

In response to the president's attack, NFL officials, team owners, personnel, and players decided to demonstrate unity in different ways. While some teams, including the Pittsburgh Steelers, voted to stay in the tunnel during the playing of the anthem, others opted to stand arm-in-arm on the sidelines. On some teams, numerous players took a knee while their teammates and coaches stood behind them in support.

When asked about the demonstrations, Goodell attributed them to Trump's divisive rhetoric and expressed his pride in the unity and passion of players, owners, and team officials. "I spent a lot of time listening to our players and coaches and owners over the past few days. They really care about our league. I just think we need more understanding" (King 2017).

In October 2017, league officials, NFL owners, and representatives from the NFL Players' Association met to discuss the issue, concerned by declining TV ratings and attendance figures. After the meeting, Goodell announced that the league's stance was that every player should stand for the national anthem. However, players who decided to take a knee out of conscience would not be penalized.

"We want our players to stand," he said. "We're going to continue to encourage them to stand. And we're going to continue to work on these issues in the community" (Reyes 2017).

Goodell sought to find a compromise between the players and the league on the contentious issue during the remainder of the 2017 season. He argued that the players' protests were being misinterpreted and that football should avoid politics. "Players repeat over and over again this isn't about disrespect for our flag or military or our veterans. And I believe them," he stated. "But they also have to understand that it is interpreted much differently on a national basis" (Gleeson, 2017).

On May 23, 2018, NFL owners announced a new national anthem policy at the conclusion of their spring meetings. The policy requires players and team personnel to stand if they are on the field during the anthem. The league may impose a fine on teams if there is a violation. However, there is an option for players or team personnel to stay in the locker room for the playing of the national anthem.

"The policy adopted today was approved in concert with the NFL's ongoing commitment to local communities and our country—one that is extraordinary in scope, resources, and alignment with our players," Goodell stated. "We are dedicated to continuing our collaboration with players to advance the goals of justice and fairness in all corners of our society" (Goodell 2018).

Further Reading

Gleeson, Scott. 2017. "Roger Goodell Wants NFL to Move Past Protests, Says Fans Come to Games to 'Have Fun'." *USA Today,* November 9, 2017. https://www.usatoday.com/story/sports/nfl/2017/11/09/roger-goodell-wants-nfl-move-past-anthem-protests-says-fans-come-games-to-have-fun/848325001/

Goodell, Roger. 2018. "Roger Goodell's Statement on National Anthem Policy." NFL.com, May 23, 2018. http://www.nfl.com/news/story/0ap3000000933962/article/roger-goodells-statement-on-national-anthem-policy

King, Peter. 2017. "Monday Morning QB: Response to President Trump Made Roger Goodell 'Proud of Our League'." *Sports Illustrated,* September 25,

2017. https://www.si.com/nfl/2017/09/25/nfl-anthem-protests-roger
-goodell-president-trump-week-3-peter-king

National Football League. 2016. "Goodell Recognizes Kap's Right to Protest, Dis-
agrees with Action." NFL.com, September 7, 2016. http://www.nfl.com/
news/story/0ap3000000696136/article/goodell-recognizes-kaps-right-to
-protest-disagrees-with-action

Reyes, Lorenzo. 2017. "Roger Goodell: NFL Wants 'Zero' Players to Protest during
National Anthem." *USA Today*, October 18, 2017. https://www.usatoday
.com/story/sports/nfl/2017/10/18/roger-goodell-national-anthem-protest
-nfl-kneeling/776702001/

Jenkins, Malcolm (1987–)

NFL player who knelt in protest in 2016 and cofounded the Players Coalition

Malcolm Jenkins was born on December 20, 1987, in East Orange, New Jersey. As a student at Piscataway Township High School he played wide receiver and defensive back for the school's football team, which won three consecutive state championships. After graduating from high school in 2005 he joined the Ohio State University football program, where he continued to excel. In 2006 he was voted consensus first-team All-Big Ten as a sophomore, and in 2008 he received the Jim Thorpe Award, an annual honor bestowed on college football's best defensive back.

In the 2009 NFL Draft, the New Orleans Saints selected Jenkins 14th overall. That season, the Saints achieved a 13-3 record to finish first in the NFC South, then rolled through the playoffs to earn a spot in Super Bowl XLIV in Miami, Florida. The Saints beat the Colts, 31-17, to cap a storybook rookie season for Jenkins.

In 2010, Jenkins started a nonprofit charity, The Malcolm Jenkins Foundation, to serve communities in need. The organization's mission is to "effectuate positive change in the lives of youth by providing resources, innovative opportunities, and experiences that will help them succeed in life and become contributing members of their communities" (The Malcolm Jenkins Foundation). The creation of the foundation reflected Jenkins's deep commitment to community activism, which also included hosting football camps for high school athletes in New Jersey, providing food and other resources for needy families in Ohio, and creating mentoring programs and other assistance for young people in New Orleans.

After several seasons with the Saints, Jenkins became an unrestricted free agent in 2014. He ultimately signed a three-year contract with the Philadelphia Eagles, where he continued to play at a high level. In 2016 Jenkins even earned a trip to the Pro Bowl (the NFL's all-star game) for the first time.

The 2016 football season also marked a personal turning point for Jenkins. In August 2016, Colin Kaepernick, a star quarterback for the San Francisco 49ers, began his protests during the national anthem in several preseason football contests. By September, Kaepernick's protest had evolved into kneeling during the anthem. Inspired by his actions, other players joined the protest in the following weeks.

The week before the Eagles' game against the Chicago Bears on September 19, Jenkins announced that he would be taking part in the anthem protests. He explained that he delayed taking part until after the anniversary of the September 11, 2001, terrorist attacks to avoid taking attention away from the victims' families (Reuters 2016). Subsequently, during the national anthem, Jenkins and two teammates, Ron Brooks and Steve Means, stood together and raised their fists in the air.

Jenkins continued his protest throughout the season and into the next. During this period, he became a prominent voice in the player protests. He set up a meeting with Philadelphia Police Commissioner Richard Ross and a group of NFL players to foster more communication and engagement between the two groups. On March 30, 2017, Jenkins and fellow NFL players Johnson Bademosi, Anquan Boldin, and Donte Stallworth met with members of Congress to discuss criminal justice reform. Jenkins and Boldin also cofounded The Players Coalition, a group of NFL players and owners working together to address social justice and civil rights issues important to the players. In May 2018, the NFL and the Players Coalition pledged $90 million to those efforts.

To Jenkins, the involvement of NFL players in social activism was essential. "It feels like the state of our country and where we are, it's an emergency," he commented to *USA Today*. "There's a need for people of influence and people with access to help to get involved" (Jones 2018). For his activism, Jenkins received the 2017 Byron Whizzer White Award, which is the highest honor given by the NFL Players Association to NFL players who have a profound positive effect on their team.

Jenkins continued to excel on the football field, racking up another Pro Bowl selection in 2017. That same season, the Eagles marched to Super Bowl LII in Minneapolis, Minnesota, where they defeated the New England Patriots in a 41-33 thriller.

A few months after the Eagles' big victory, on May 23, 2018, the NFL owners announced new rules requiring players and team personnel to stand if they are on the field during the playing of the nation anthem. However, the policy does provide the option for players to remain in the locker room at that time if they prefer. If a player or other team personnel violates the policy, the team may be subject to a fine by the NFL.

On Instagram, Jenkins criticized the changes to the policy. "What the NFL owners did today was thwart the players' constitutional rights to express themselves and use our platform to draw attention to social injustices like racial inequality in our country. Everyone loses when voices get stifled" (@malcolmjenkins27 May 23, 2018).

In early June, further controversy erupted when President Donald Trump called off the traditional White House celebration to honor the Philadelphia Eagles for their Super Bowl championship. The president cancelled the event, scheduled for June 5, the day after news leaked out that several prominent players would not attend. They objected to the idea of attending an event hosted by Trump, who had previously condemned NFL players who knelt or engaged in other forms of peaceful protest during the national anthem as unpatriotic.

President Trump framed the cancellation as a necessary response to the team's lack of patriotism. "[The Philadelphia Eagles] disagree with their president because he insists that they proudly stand for the National Anthem, hand on heart, in honor of the great men and women of our military and the people of our country. The Eagles wanted to send a smaller delegation, but the 1,000 fans planning to attend deserve better" (Trump 2018).

In a response posted on Twitter the next day, Jenkins objected to the president's statement. He asserted that the players' social justice activism and community involvement was a sign of their patriotism and he described efforts to paint them as unpatriotic by Trump and other critics as dishonest. "We do it [engage in symbolic protests during the anthem] because we love this country and our community," Jenkins posted. "Everyone, regardless of race or socioeconomic status, deserves to be treated equally. We are fighting for racial and social equality." Jenkins also pointed out that no members of the Eagles knelt during the anthem at any point during the 2017 season, despite Trump's insinuation. "Instead, the decision was made to lie, and paint the picture that these players are anti-America, anti-flag, and anti-military" (@MalcolmJenkins June 5, 2018).

Jenkins continued his activism into the 2018 NFL season. Before the start of the Eagles' preseason game with the Pittsburgh Steelers on August 9, 2018, Jenkins and a teammate, De'Vante Bausby, raised their fists during the national anthem. A week later, Jenkins and Bausby stood in the tunnel, while another teammate, Michael Bennett, opted to remain in the locker room during the national anthem. Jenkins also stood in the tunnel for the next few preseason games against the Cleveland Browns and the New York Jets.

"I think it's important that we continue to keep this conversation going, that we don't let it get stagnant," Jenkins explained. "As we understand it, everyone is kind of waiting to see what the league is going to do. That doesn't mean that we stop what we've been standing up for. That's just my personal decision to make sure we keep these things in the forefront" (Folley 2018).

Further Reading

Folley, Aris. 2018. "Eagles Players Continue National Anthem Protests by Staying Off Field." *The Hill,* August 24, 2018. http://thehill.com/blogs/blog -briefing-room/news/403422-eagles-players-continue-national-anthem -protests-by-staying-off

Jenkins, Malcolm (@malcolmjenkins27). 2018. Instagram photo, May 23, 2018. https://www.instagram.com/p/BjIoflshuj8/?utm_source=ig_embed

Jenkins, Malcolm (@MalcolmJenkins). 2018. Twitter, June 5, 2018. https:// twitter.com/MalcolmJenkins/status/1004049505812172800

Jones, Leslie. 2018. "Eagles' Malcolm Jenkins Finds Voice through Social Move- ment after Leading by Example." *USA Today,* February 1, 2018. https:// www.usatoday.com/story/sports/nfl/eagles/2018/02/01/eagles-malcolm -jenkins-find-voice-through-social-movements-after-leading-example/ 1088645001

The Malcolm Jenkins Foundation. 2018. http://malcolmjenkins27.com/bio/

Reuters. "Eagles Players Latest to Join Anthem Protest." *Reuters,* September 19, 2016. https://www.reuters.com/article/us-nfl-anthem-eagles-idUSKCN11Q07I

Trump, Donald. 2018. "Statement by the President." June 4, 2018. https:// www.whitehouse.gov/briefings-statements/statement-by-the-president-2/

Johnson, Christopher (1959–)

Chairman and CEO of the New York Jets who chose not to fine or suspend protesting players

Christopher Johnson was born in 1959. His great-grandfather, Robert Wood Johnson, was one of the cofounders of Johnson & Johnson, a phar- maceutical and manufacturing corporation established in 1886 in New Jersey. During the twentieth century, the company amassed a fortune by manufacturing, distributing, and selling pharmaceuticals, first aid products, beauty products, biomedical devices, and a number of other products. Today, the company owns more than 250 subsidiary companies. It reported $76.5 billion in worldwide sales in 2017 (Johnson & Johnson, 2018).

The worldwide success of the Johnson & Johnson company allowed later generations of the family to devote themselves to worthy philanthropic, business, political, and social causes. Christopher's older brother, Robert

Wood "Woody" Johnson IV, established himself as a businessman, political fundraiser, and philanthropist before purchasing an NFL team, the New York Jets, in 2000 for $635 million. In 2017, the team was valued at $2.75 billion (*Forbes* 2018).

Woody Johnson's involvement in Republican politics and his support of Donald Trump in the 2016 U.S. presidential election led to his nomination to become the United States ambassador to the United Kingdom in early 2017. In June of that same year, the New York Jets announced that if the Senate confirmed Johnson's nomination, Christopher Johnson would take over as Chairman and CEO of the team. In that position, Christopher would solely oversee the day-to-day operations while Woody functioned in his new diplomatic role.

"The New York Jets have been an integral part of our family since 2000, but this is a unique opportunity for Woody," explained Christopher Johnson in a statement. "His patriotism and commitment to our country have always been a passion of his. Over the years, we have learned that ownership of the New York Jets is a special responsibility. Personally, if Woody is nominated and confirmed, I would be honored to oversee the organization, continuing to build a team on and off the field that our fans are proud of and deserve" (NFL.com 2017).

The Senate confirmed Woody's nomination in August 2017, officially handing over the day-to-day responsibilities to his brother. To the press, Christopher clarified his role for fans and other observers. "I'm in touch with him constantly, but none of it is about football," Christopher explained to reporters. "Over the years he has always bounced things off of me, and it would be great if I could do that with him. But he really has a full-time job over there. We are not discussing football. He's out of it" (Vasquez 2017).

Christopher Johnson's thoughtful, hands-on management style quickly elicited praise from players, reporters, and colleagues. Reporters noted that he made a point to eat with players and team personnel, watch practices on a regular basis, and take an interest in issues important to players. This was reportedly in contrast to his brother's management style and made Christopher more accessible to players than his brother. "It makes him real, it makes him human, not just a figure," explained Jets player Demario Davis. "When you see him, he's somebody you want to go up to and shake his hand and talk to. It's not just a team owner-player conversation, it's real life" (Cimini 2017).

One of Johnson's priorities has been to meet with players and listen to their concerns on a regular basis. He also displayed a genuine interest in educating himself about the issues and causes that interest them. On December 19, 2017, for example, Johnson accompanied three Jets players—Kelvin Beachum, Demario Davis, and Josh McCown—for an all-day meeting with the Bronx Public Defender's Office in an effort to learn more about racial disparities and bias in the U.S. legal system.

As the controversy over the NFL anthem protests grew during 2017, Johnson's rapport with the players turned out to be a valuable asset. Before the September 24 game between the Jets and Miami Dolphins, Johnson met individually with players to ask them if he could stand with them during the national anthem. Players were impressed by the gesture and his emphasis on team unity. As Jets player Steve McLendon noted, "Him standing with us means a lot. It shows he's with us" (Cimini 2017).

On May 23, 2018, the NFL owners announced a new national anthem policy mandating that players and team personnel stand if they are on the field during the anthem. The players, however, have the option to remain in the locker room if they prefer. According to the policy, the league may impose fines on any team whose players or personnel violate the new rule.

In an interview with *Newsday,* Johnson explained he voted to approve the changes to the policy but reaffirmed his support of the players' right to protest without fear of retaliation. "I seriously struggled with this," he asserted. "In the end, I felt I had to support it from a membership standpoint" (Glauber 2018).

Johnson also announced, however, that the team would pay the fines of any player fined for exercising their freedom of speech. "I never want to put restrictions on the speech of our players," he explained. "Do I prefer that they stand? Of course. But I understand if they feel the need to protest. There are some big, complicated issues that we're all struggling with, and our players are on the front lines. I don't want to come down on them like a ton of bricks, and I won't. There will be no club fines or suspensions or any sort of repercussions. If the team gets fined, that's just something I'll have to bear" (Glauber 2018).

Johnson's position on the new NFL policy was supported by his players and many fans, who felt he stood with his team and supported the players' right to protest. Not everyone saw Johnson's stance as an admirable one, however. Critics said his decision encouraged an atmosphere of anti-Americanism and disrespect for the military and law enforcement officers.

Further Reading

Cimini, Rich. 2017. "Jets' Camera-Shy Owner Stands with His Players . . . on and off the Field." ESPN, December 29, 2017. http://www.espn.com/blog/new-york-jets/post/_/id/73830/jets-camera-shy-owner-stands-with-his-players-on-and-off-the-field

Forbes. 2018. "The World's Most Valuable Sports Teams." *Forbes,* 2018. https://www.forbes.com/sites/forbespr/2018/07/18/forbes-releases-2018-list-of-the-worlds-most-valuable-sports-teams/#ede03e175ff8Glauber, Bob. 2018. "Jets Chairman Christopher Johnson Backs Players' Right to Protest." *News day,* May 23, 2018. https://www.newsday.com/sports/football/jets/national-anthem-christopher-johnson-fines-1.18700702

Johnson & Johnson. 2018. "What You Need to Know about Johnson & Johnson's 2017 Full Year Earnings Report," January 23, 2018. https://www.jnj.com/latest-news/what-you-need-to-know-about-johnson-johnsons-2017-full-year-earnings-report

NFL. 2017. "Trump to Nominate Jets' Johnson as US Ambassador." NFL.com, June 22, 2017. http://www.nfl.com/news/story/0ap3000000817147/article/trump-to-nominate-jets-johnson-as-us-ambassador

Vasquez, Andy. 2017. "Christopher Johnson Making All Decisions for Jets, Woody Johnson Is 'Out'." *North Jersey,* September 20, 2017. https://www.northjersey.com/story/sports/nfl/jets/2017/09/20/christopher-johnson-making-all-decisions-jets-woody-johnson-out/685838001/

Jones, Jerry (1942–)

Owner, president, and general manager of the Dallas Cowboys who claimed NFL protests negatively affect the league

On October 13, 1942, Jerry Jones was born in Los Angeles, California. A few years after his birth, his family moved to North Little Rock, Arkansas, where he spent the rest of his childhood. Jones was a highly regarded running back on his high school football team, and in 1960 he accepted a football scholarship at the University of Arkansas. As a senior, was a cocaptain of the Arkansas Razorbacks squad, which won the NCAA National Championship in 1964.

After graduating from college, Jones joined his parents in Springfield, Missouri, where his father had established a successful insurance company. Jones worked at the company for a time as an executive vice president before venturing out on his own. He eventually established Jones Oil and Land Lease, an oil and gas exploration business based in Arkansas. The company expanded rapidly, establishing Jones as a force in the industry and eventually providing him with the financial resources to fulfill his long-time dream of owning an NFL team.

In 1989, Jones bought the Dallas Cowboys, one of the NFL's flagship franchises, for $140 million. He quickly set out to improve the financial situation of the team, which had been losing $1 million a month. Jones cut overhead, secured lucrative sponsorships, and created other streams of revenue. In a controversial move, he also replaced the team's legendary coach,

Tom Landry and its longtime general manager, Tex Schramm. He established himself as the head of the club's football operations.

Although fans and sports journalists criticized these moves, they proved beneficial. The Cowboys won the Super Bowl at the close of the 1992, 1993, and 1995 seasons, a performance that led many observers to laud Jones's club as the best NFL team of the 1990s. Since that time, the Cowboys have remained one of the most profitable and popular teams in the league, despite a two-decade drought of Super Bowl appearances.

In 2017, Jones was elected to the Pro Football Hall of Fame in recognition of his leadership of the Cowboys. In his induction speech, Jones attributed his love for the game to the respect of his teammates and the lessons it taught him. "It's a place where you can make the block football, you can make the block in the line, nobody in the world knows about it, but the next day when you hit the film, your teammates do," he said. "And you can look in the mirror and you can feel as good as if you'd made six touchdowns the night before. That's football" (Professional Football Hall of Fame 2017).

When the player-led protests of racism and police brutality broke out in 2016, Jones and other NFL owners faced a public relations crisis. The controversy began in September, when Colin Kaepernick, a quarterback with the San Francisco 49ers, decided to protest recent incidents of police brutality and ongoing institutionalized racial inequality by kneeling during the playing of the national anthem before a 49ers game. Other players were inspired by his actions and joined the protest in ensuing weeks.

On September 22, 2017, President Donald Trump brought the issue into the national spotlight when he harshly criticized and insulted the protesters during a rally in Alabama, calling them unpatriotic and disrespectful. Moreover, he urged NFL owners to fire any player participating in the protests.

Two days later, Jones, his sons Stephen and Jerry Jr., and his daughter Charlotte all joined the team's players, coaches, and staff on the field before a game against the Arizona Cardinals. They locked arms together in an expression of unity, and they all knelt before the anthem and stood during the anthem.

At the post-game press conference, Jones described the team's actions as a response to the president's fiery words. "We planned and it was executed according to plan that we would go out and kneel in prayer, or kneel or basically stand and make the statement regarding the need for unity and the need for equality," he explained to reporters. "And that big American flag, it came down on the field, and we all stood toes-out on the field and recognized and respected the American flag and the national anthem. So it was a coordinated effort" (Bieler et al. 2017).

However, when the controversy continued to gather steam over the next few weeks, Jones became the first NFL owner to come out and take a strong stand against kneeling. He vowed to bench any player that would not stand during the national anthem. "I am very supportive of the team, but under no circumstances will the Dallas Cowboys—I don't care what happens—under no circumstances will we as an organization, coaches, players, not support and stand and recognize and honor the flag. Period" (Archer 2017).

Although many fans and commentators applauded Jones's statement as strong and patriotic, others denounced the position he adopted. James Ragland, an editorial writer for the *Dallas News,* charged that "What we are seeing is plantation politics at its finest: A ruling class of wealthy white owners—with Jones as its front man—unwilling to meet black players halfway. . . . Instead of falling into President Donald Trump's trap—turning a benign and peaceful protest into cannon fodder for America's culture war—Jones would've been wiser to use his negotiating skills to strike a substantive compromise" (Ragland 2017).

Jones's tough stance and emphasis on team unity had an effect. During the 2017 season, no Dallas Cowboy player knelt or sat during the playing of the national anthem.

Behind the scenes, though, Jones and other NFL owners decided that they needed to create a stronger policy on the NFL anthem protests. In a court deposition, Jones, a close friend and supporter of President Trump, revealed that the president told him the NFL would not win on the issue and pressured him to implement a tougher policy. Also, Jones and other owners expressed concern that public opposition to the protests could be seen in diminished fan attendance.

Alarmed, Jones declared that the protests were having a negative effect on the league. "At times, if I am anything, I am first and foremost a proponent of making the NFL strong. Making us have as many people watching the game as we can and watching in light of what we are doing and that's playing football," Jones contended. "If all this makes you stronger to represent messages, let's don't do it in a way that tears down the strength of the NFL" (Hill 2017).

On May 23, 2018, the NFL owners announced that they had approved a new national anthem policy that requires players and team personnel to stand if they are on the field during the anthem. However, the policy does provide the option for the players to remain in the locker room at that time if they prefer. If a player or other team personnel violates the policy, the team may be subject to a fine.

Further Reading

Archer, Todd. 2017. "Jerry Jones: Cowboys Will Bench Any Player Who 'Disrespects' Flag." ESPN, October 9, 2017. http://www.espn.com/nfl/story/_/id/20961541/dallas-cowboys-owner-jerry-jones-says-player-disrespects-flag-playhttp://www.espn.com/nfl/story/_/id/20961541/dallas-cowboys-owner-jerry-jones-says-player-disrespects-flag-play

Bieler, Dez, Mark Maske, and Cindy Boren. 2017. "'Trump Can't Divide This': Cowboys, along with Owner Jerry Jones, Kneel before Anthem in Arizona." *The Washington Post*, September 26, 2017. https://www.washingtonpost.com/news/early-lead/wp/2017/09/25/cowboys-players-take-a-knee-with-owner-jerry-jones-before-standing-for-anthem/?utm_term=.a2f9d86ad168

Hill, Clarence E., Jr. 2017. "Cowboys Owner Jerry Jones Says the NFL Is Being Damaged by Protests." *Fort Worth Star-Telegram,* October 22, 2017. http://www.star-telegram.com/sports/nfl/dallas-cowboys/article180344236.html

Jones, Jerry. 2017. "Jerry Jones Enshrinement Speech." *Pro Football Hall of Fame,* August 5, 2017. http://www.profootballhof.com/players/jerry-jones/enshrinement/

Ragland, James. 2017. "A Lesson in Plantation Politics from Dallas Cowboys Owner Jerry Jones." *Dallas News,* October 11, 2017. https://www.dallasnews.com/opinion/commentary/2017/10/11/lesson-plantation-politics-dallas-cowboys-owner-jerry-jones

Kaepernick, Colin (1987–)

Former NFL player and the first player to kneel in protest during the National Anthem

Colin Kaepernick was born on November 3, 1987, in Milwaukee, Wisconsin. He grew up in Turlock, California, where he excelled at sports, particularly football, basketball, and baseball. In 2007, Kaepernick was offered a football scholarship to the University of Nevada in Reno. During his freshman season, he got a chance to start as quarterback and made the most of it. Over his college career, he set several school and divisional records, including becoming the first quarterback in Division 1 Football Bowl Subdivision (FBS) to pass for more than 10,000 yards and run for more than 4,000 yards in his career.

The San Francisco 49ers picked Kaepernick in the second round of the 2011 NFL Draft. That season he primarily served as a back-up quarterback, but earned a starting role during the 2012 season. The team advanced through the playoffs that year, but it lost to the Baltimore Ravens in Super Bowl XLVII.

Off the field, Kaepernick's social justice activism became a feature on his social media accounts, particularly his outrage over the killings of unarmed

African Americans during encounters with law enforcement. After the death of Alton Sterling, a young black man shot by two police officers in Baton Rouge, Louisiana, on June 5, 2016, Kaepernick expressed his anger on Instagram. "This is what lynchings look like in 2016!" he posted. "Another murder in the streets because the color of a man's skin, at the hands of people who say they will protect us" (@kaepernick7, July 6, 2016).

During the first few preseason games of the 2016 season, Kaepernick sat on the bench during the national anthem. His actions did not attract much attention; he was not in uniform for the game and did not speak to the press about it. At the end of August, however, the press took notice. "I am not going to stand up to show pride in a flag for a country that oppresses black people and people of color," Kaepernick explained. "To me, this is bigger than football and it would be selfish on my part to look the other way. There are bodies on the street and people getting paid leave and getting away with murder" (Wyche 2016).

Kaepernick vowed to continue his protests until there was social justice reform. "I'm going to continue to stand with the people that are being oppressed. To this is something that has to change. When there's significant change and I feel that flag represents what it's supposed to represent, this country is representing people the way that it's supposed to, I'll stand" (Biderman 2016).

On August 30, former NFL player and military veteran Nate Boyer published an open letter to Kaepernick in the *Army Times*. Boyer expressed his admiration for Kaepernick's courage but disagreed with his methods. Boyer argued that sitting on the bench during the national anthem implied disrespect for soldiers and their sacrifices.

After reading Boyer's letter, Kaepernick met with him before the next game to find ways to protest without dishonoring those who have served the country. Boyer suggested kneeling, or taking a knee, during the anthem, which is a gesture of respect to a fallen soldier. In that way, it would function as a compromise and signal regard for the military. During the playing of the national anthem before the game that day, Kaepernick and teammate Eric Reid took a knee, while Boyer stood alongside them with his hand over his heart.

For Kaepernick, the controversy over the protests served a purpose. "I love America, I love people. That's why I'm doing this," he pointed out in the postgame press conference. "I want to help make America better. I think having these conversations helps everybody have a better understanding of where everybody is coming from. Those conversations are important to have, because the better we understand each other, the better we know each other, the better we can deal and communicate with each other, which ultimately makes everyone, puts everybody in a better position" (Wagoner 2016).

During that same press conference, he announced that he would be donating the first $1 million of his salary that year to organizations that work in disadvantaged communities. He fulfilled that pledge in 2018, with the funds being distributed through the Colin Kaepernick Foundation, which states its mission as "to fight oppression of all kinds globally, through education and social activism" (Colin Kaepernick Foundation 2018).

The protests continued throughout the 2016 season, spreading to other sporting leagues and athletic competitions. It did spark debates about patriotism, racial equality, criminal justice reform, and police brutality. Kaepernick became a flashpoint for the controversy, considered a hero to many but a villain to others. When attendance numbers and TV ratings fell flat, many NFL owners and league officials pointed to the controversy over the protests and the efficacy of fan and sponsor boycotts as one of the main reasons for the game's declining popularity.

After the 2016 season, Kaepernick opted out of his contract and became a free agent. He went unsigned throughout the 2017 season, leading many to believe that NFL owners blacklisted him for his leading role in the protests. NFL officials denied it.

The theory that Kaepernick had been blacklisted gained credibility, however, when President Trump took credit for Kaepernick's unemployment during a speech in Louisville, Kentucky, in March 2017. "There was an article today, it was reported, that NFL owners don't want to pick him up because they don't want to get a nasty tweet from Donald Trump," he boasted (Jenkins 2017).

In November 2017, Kaepernick filed a grievance against the NFL, alleging that the owners colluded to keep him out of the league. In a statement, Kaepernick's attorney, Mark Geragos, outlined the reasons for the filing. "If the NFL (as well as all professional sports teams) is to remain a meritocracy, then principled and peaceful protest—which the owners themselves made great theater imitating weeks ago—should not be punished and athletes should not be denied employment based on partisan political provocation by the Executive Branch of our government," the statement read. "Such a precedent threatens all patriotic Americans and hearkens back to our darkest days as a nation. Protecting all athletes from such collusive conduct is what compelled Mr. Kaepernick to file his grievance" (ESPN 2017).

In April 2018, Kaepernick was named Amnesty International's Ambassador of Conscience Award winner. In his acceptance speech, he traced the reasons for his social justice activism. "While taking a knee is a physical display that challenges the merits of who is excluded from the notion of freedom, liberty, and justice for all, the protest is also rooted in a convergence of my moralistic beliefs, and my love for the people," he explained. "Seeking the truth, finding the truth, telling the truth and living the truth has been, and always will be what guides my actions. For as long as I have a beating heart, I will continue on this path, working on behalf of the people" (Kaepernick 2018).

In August 2018, an arbitrator, Stephen Burbank, ruled that Kaepernick's collusion claim would proceed to a hearing unless a settlement could be negotiated between the NFL and Kaepernick. Legal experts pointed to the ground-breaking nature of the decision; if it was found that 14 or more teams colluded to deprive Kaepernick out of his right to collective bargain with an NFL team, then the Collective Bargaining Agreement (CBA), a labor agreement that governs the relationship between owners and players, could be terminated.

In early September, Nike revealed the newest ad in the brand's iconic "just do it" campaign. It featured a close-up photograph of Colin Kaepernick's face with the message "Believe in something. Even if it means sacrificing everything. Just do it." To many, the message referred to the prevailing belief that Kaepernick remained unsigned by an NFL team because of his leading role in the NFL protests.

Nike touted Kaepernick as a role model for its customers. "We believe Colin is one of the most inspirational athletes of this generation, who has leveraged the power of sport to help move the world forward," stated Gino Fisanotti, Nike's vice president of brand for North America. "We wanted to energize its meaning and introduce 'Just Do It' to a new generation of athletes" (Rovell 2018).

The ad generated backlash from NFL fans who opposed the protests. Some posted videos online of burning Nike products, others vowed to boycott the brand in the future. It also inspired support from other pro athletes, like tennis legend Serena Williams and basketball star LeBron James.

Many commentators found Nike's ad to be provocative, but regarded it as a good business move. "Nike had to have known that the ad would not be taken well by some, but it decided to release it anyway. A brand as big as Nike doesn't make big moves like this without considering every angle. By at least one measure, the ad was extremely successful. Nike and its ad were top-trending terms on Twitter Monday [September 3] when it was released. At the very least, everyone is talking about it" (Green 2018).

The day after the ad's release, Trump criticized Nike for sending "a terrible message." He added, "As much as I disagree with the Colin Kaepernick endorsement, in another way—I mean, I wouldn't have done it. In another way, it is what the country is all about, that you have certain freedoms to do things that other people think you shouldn't do, but I am personally on another side of it" (Coglianese and Enjeti 2018).

Further Reading

Biderman, Chris. 2016. "Transcript: Colin Kaepernick Addresses Sitting during National Anthem." *USA Today*, August 28, 2016. https://ninerswire .usatoday.com/2016/08/28/transcript-colin-kaepernick-addresses-sitting -during-national-anthem/

Coglianese, Vince, and Saagar Enjeti. 2018. "Trump Critical, but Says Nike's Kaepernick Deal Is 'What This Country Is All about'." *Daily Caller,* September 4, 2018. https://dailycaller.com/2018/09/04/trump-interview-nike-kaepernick -deal/

Colin Kaepernick Foundation, 2018. www.kaepernick7.com

ESPN. 2017. "QB Colin Kaepernick Files Grievance for Collusion against NFL Owners." ESPN, October 15, 2017. https://abcnews.go.com/Sports/qb -colin-kaepernick-files-grievance-collusion-nfl-owners/story?id=50499785

Green, Dennis. 2018. "Nike Ignited a Firestorm of Fury with Its New Colin Kaepernick Ad, but It's Still a Brilliant Strategy." *Business Insider,* September 4, 2018. https://www.businessinsider.com/nike-colin-kaepernick-deal -strategy-2018-9?r=UK&IR=T

Jenkins, Aric. 2017. "President Trump Says NFL Teams Fear a 'Nasty Tweet' from Him If They Sign Colin Kaepernick." *Time,* March 21, 2017. http:// time.com/4707742/president-trump-colin-kaepernick/

Kaepernick, Colin (@kaepernick7). 2016. Instagram video, July 6, 2016. https:// www.instagram.com/p/BHhetl8g_EE/

Kaepernick, Colin. 2018. "Amnesty International's Ambassador of Conscience Award: Transcript of Speech." *Amnesty International,* April 21, 2018. https://www.amnesty.nl/content/uploads/2018/04/Colin-Kaepernicks -Speech-Ambassador-of-Conscience-Final.pdf?x66178

Rovell, Darren. 2018. "Colin Kaepernick's Part of Nike's 30th Anniversary of 'Just Do It' Campaign." ESPN, September 3, 2018. http://www.espn.com/nfl/ story/_/id/24568359/colin-kaepernick-face-nike-just-do-30th-anniversary -campaign

Wagoner, Nick. 2016. "Transcript of Colin Kaepernick's Comments after Preseason Finale." ESPN, September 2, 2016. http://www.espn.com/blog/san -francisco-49ers/post/_/id/19126/transcript-of-colin-kaepernicks -comments-after-preseason-finale

Wyche, Steve. 2016. "Colin Kaepernick Explains Why He Sat during National Anthem." NFL.com, August 28, 2016. http://www.nfl.com/news/story/ 0ap3000000691077/article/colin-kaepernick-explains-protest-of-national -anthem

Kraft, Robert (1941–)

New England Patriots owner who supported players' right to protest but remained concerned about financial implications for the league

Robert "Bob" Kraft was born on June 5, 1941, in Brookline, Massachusetts. He attended Columbia University in New York City, where he was elected senior class president. He went on to attain an MBA from Harvard Business School in 1965.

After briefly considering a career in politics, Kraft joined the Rand-Whitney group, a packaging company located in Worcester, Massachusetts. Within a few years, he became the company chairman. In 1972, he started International Forest Products, a company specializing in forest products trading and paper products manufacturing. As Kraft's business interests continued to expand, he formed the Kraft Group in 1998. Today, the conglomerate is also involved in real estate development, construction, private equity and venture investing, and philanthropic activities.

In 1974, Kraft was part of a group that purchased the Boston Lobsters, a professional tennis team in the World Team Tennis league. Although the Boston Lobsters folded in 1978, Kraft remained interested in team ownership, making a couple of unsuccessful attempts to purchase the New England Patriots. In 1994, Kraft offered $172 million for the team, which at the time was the highest price paid for any NFL franchise. Kraft's bid was accepted, launching an era of unrivaled success for the team on and off the field. During Kraft's ownership, the Patriots have consistently made the NFL playoffs and are five-time Super Bowl champions. For many, the Patriots are the gold standard for professional football in the early twenty-first century. Today, the team is valued at $3.7 billion, making it one of the most valuable franchises in sports (Badenhausen 2017).

The controversy over the NFL anthem protests, however, posed a threat to the success of the NFL and teams like the Patriots. During the 2016 preseason, Colin Kaepernick, quarterback for the San Francisco 49ers, began to demonstrate against social and racial injustice by sitting, then kneeling, during the playing of the national anthem. Over the ensuing weeks, a few teammates and players on other teams joined the protests, which started to gain nationwide attention and continued into the following season.

During a September 2017 rally in Alabama, President Donald Trump condemned protesters, calling the players unpatriotic and disrespectful to the flag and the nation's military. He also urged NFL owners to fire any player participating in the protests.

On the team's Twitter account, Kraft responded to the president, his long-time friend, a few days later. "I am deeply disappointed by the tone of the comments made by the President on Friday," the statement read. "I am proud to be associated with so many players who make such tremendous contributions in positively impacting our communities. Their efforts, both on and off the field, help bring people together and make our community stronger.

"There is no greater unifier in our country than sports, and unfortunately, nothing more divisive than politics. I think our political leaders could learn a lot from the lessons of teamwork and the importance of working together toward a common goal. Our players are intelligent, thoughtful and care deeply about our community and I support their right to peacefully affect social change and raise awareness in a manner that they feel is most impactful" (@Patriots September 24, 2017).

President Trump responded. "Look, he has to take his ideas and go with what he wants. I think it's very disrespectful to our country. I think it's very, very disrespectful to our flag. So, he's a good friend of mine and I want him to do what he wants to do, but we have a great country, we have great people representing our country, especially our soldiers, our first responders and they should be treated with respect. And when you get on your knee and you don't respect the American flag or the anthem, that's not being treated with respect" (Tynes 2017).

The controversy simmered throughout the season, and Kraft continued to support his players. "I think that there were some comments made about what our young men were doing that were a little inflammatory and inappropriate, and I thought I had to speak out," he said. "I spoke to the team, and I told them that they were free to do what they thought was correct as long—I try to bring unity and bring things together, and part of that is respecting how other people think" (Jennings 2017).

In October, owners, league executives, and several players held a confidential meeting to discuss the matter. Afterward, an audiotape featuring Kraft's comments about Trump's rhetoric and motives leaked to the press. "The problem we have is, we will have a president who will use that as fodder to do his mission that I don't feel is in the best interests of America," Kraft said during the meeting. "It's divisive and it's horrible" (Belson and Leibovich 2018).

By the end of the 2017–2018 season, NFL owners were determined to move past the controversy by crafting a stronger NFL anthem protest policy. Kraft expressed his optimism such an effort could bring owners, players, and league executives together on the issue. "I heard there's a heightened awareness among ownership in the league, and I think players and owners understand what this means to our total business in trying to come together in a way that I hope is very positive" (Volin 2018).

In May 2018, the NFL owners announced a new national anthem policy that requires players and team personnel to stand if they are on the field during the anthem. If the policy is violated, the team may be subject to a fine by the league. There is, however, an option for players or team personnel to stay in the locker room for the national anthem if an individual chooses to do so.

Further Reading

Badenhausen, Kurt. 2017. "Full List: The World's 50 Most Valuable Sports Teams 2017." *Forbes,* July 12, 2017. https://www.forbes.com/sites/kurtbadenhau sen/2017/07/12/full-list-the-worlds-50-most-valuable-sports-teams-2017/ #580482434a05

Belson, Ken, and Mark Leibovich. 2018. "Inside the Confidential NFL Meeting to Discuss National Anthem Protests." *New York Times,* April 25, 2018. https://www.nytimes.com/2018/04/25/sports/nfl-owners-kaepernick.html? smid=tw-nytsports&smtyp=cur

Jennings, Patrick. 2017. "Colin Kaepernick: From One Man Kneeling to a Movement Dividing a Country." *BBC,* October 11, 2017. https://www.bbc.com/ sport/american-football/41530732

New England Patriots (@Patriots). 2017. "Statement from Patriots Chairman & CEO Robert Kraft." Twitter, September 24, 2017. https://twitter.com/Patri ots/status/911926759590957056

Tynes, Tyler. 2017. "Donald Trump Says His Comments on NFL Player Protest 'Have Nothing to Do about Race'." *SB Nation* (blog), September 24, 2017. https://www.sbnation.com/2017/9/24/16358682/donald-trump-says-nfl -protest-anthem-race

Volin, Ben. 2018. "NFL Teams Face Fines over National Anthem Protests under New Policy." *Boston Globe,* May 23, 2018. https://www.bostonglobe.com/ sports/patriots/2018/05/23/nfl-owners-discussing-ways-handle-national -anthem-protests/F6qhnPxjUcRX6y97Bg5ddJ/story.html

Long, Chris (1985–)

First white NFL player to participate in protests during the National Anthem

On March 28, 1985, Chris Long was born in Santa Monica, California. His father, Howie Long, is a former NFL player with the Oakland Raiders and a member of the Pro Football Hall of Fame. Chris attended high school in Charlottesville, Virginia, where he helped his school football team win a state championship in his senior year. Ranked as one of the top defensive linemen in his class, he was highly recruited to play college football. At the University of Virginia, his success on the field continued. In 2007, Long was designated a first-team All-American and won the Hendricks Award, given to the best collegiate defensive end in the nation.

The then-St. Louis Rams selected Long with the second overall pick of the 2008 NFL Draft. Despite injuries, he experienced much success over a number of seasons with the team. After being released by the Rams in February 2016, Long signed a one-year deal with the New England Patriots. He subsequently helped lift the Patriots to a 14-2 regular season record. After a successful playoff run, the team celebrated an exciting comeback victory against the Atlanta Falcons in Super Bowl LI in Houston, Texas, winning with a score of 34-28.

Long switched teams again in March 2017, when he signed with the Philadelphia Eagles. Once again, events proved that he had made a wise choice in teams. Bolstered by a swarming defense of which Long was an important part, the Eagles cruised through the regular season and playoffs before defeating the New England Patriots 41-33 in Super Bowl LII.

Long's popularity in Philadelphia received a boost at midseason of the 2017 campaign when he announced that he would be donating his entire annual salary to educational charities in Charlottesville, St. Louis, Boston, and Philadelphia, all cities where he had played football. "I'm playing the entire 2017 season without collecting income because I believe that education is the best gateway to a better tomorrow for everyone in America" (Mather 2017).

By that time, Long was already well known for his philanthropy as well as his social and political activism. In 2015, for example, he started the Waterboys Initiative in response to his experiences during a climbing expedition to Mt. Kilimanjaro a few years before. During the trip, he had learned that many of the rural communities in the region suffered from a lack of clean water. The aim of Waterboys is to help Worldserve, an organization that builds clean water wells for the people of Tanzania and other communities in East Africa. He expanded his philanthropic efforts by establishing the Chris Long Foundation in 2015. Its mission is to improve access to clean water worldwide, fight homelessness, and support military veterans and children in need.

In August 2017, Long vocally condemned violence committed by far-right activists at the Unite the Right rally in his former hometown of Charlottesville, Virginia. The rally brought together alt-right activists, white supremacists, and neo-Nazi elements in opposition to the removal of a statue of Confederate general Robert E. Lee from a local park. Tragedy struck when one of the far-right activists purposely drove into a group of counter protesters, killing a young woman and injuring many others.

On Twitter and in interviews, Long denounced the violence of the rally, the openly racist and anti-Semitic ideology of many of the attendees, and the refusal of Donald Trump to strongly condemn the far-right marchers. "You can say what you want about the president's remarks," he said in an interview. "I wish he'd categorically spoken out against white supremacy" (Hayes 2017).

Long's outspoken reaction to the Charlottesville rally and its aftermath sparked controversy with some fans who told him to keep his opinions to himself. For Long, however, speaking out was the right thing to do. "Some people are tired of hearing me tweet because they want me to stick to football but I like to use social media like I was a regular guy because I think I am," Long asserted. "I don't tell people to stick to their job when they want to talk politics. And this isn't political. This is right or wrong. That's the thing. Everybody is trying to turn this political. I believe you're on one side or the other. For me, being from Charlottesville, no one wants to see you sit idly by and watch that stuff happen and not say anything" (Zangaro 2017).

Just a few days after his remarks on Charlottesville, Long made another statement when he became the first white player to actively participate in the NFL anthem demonstrations against racial injustice and police bias and brutality. During the national anthem before the Eagles' preseason game on August 17, 2017, Long put his arm around a black teammate, Malcolm Jenkins, who had raised his fist in the air as a protest.

After the game, Long explained his actions. "I've heard a lot of people say, 'Why do athletes get involved in the national anthem protests?' I've said before that I'll never kneel for an anthem because the flag means something different for everybody in this country, but I support my peers. If you don't see why you need allies for people that are fighting for equality right now, I don't think you'll ever see it. Malcolm is a leader and I'm here to show support as a white athlete" (Kulp 2017).

Long claims that his social and political sensibilities can be attributed to his football experiences. "I really do believe, it might be a cliché, but we come from a lot of different walks of life and backgrounds and I've played with a lot of guys I probably would never have met in other walks of life," he noted in 2017. "We sit here in a bubble in a really positive way. I wish the rest of the world could be on a team. I know that sounds kinds of cliché but we really get to be exposed to each other's different cultures, different ways of life and the way we look differently at things. And I think that's the really cool thing about being on a team" (Zangaro 2017).

On May 23, 2018, the NFL owners announced a new national anthem policy, which would require players and team personnel to stand if they are on the field during the anthem. The team may be subject to a fine if there is a violation. However, there is an option for players or team personnel to stay in the locker room during the playing of the national anthem if they so choose.

In a tweet later that day, Long argued that the owners put the new policy in place not out of patriotism, but because they had been pressured by President Trump and were fearful of losing business in the long run. "This is a fear of a diminished bottom line," he posted. "It's also a fear of a president turning his base against a corporation. This isn't patriotism. Don't get it confused. These owners don't love America more than the players demonstrating and taking real action to improve it" (@JOEL9ONE May 23, 2018).

Just a few weeks later, the White House celebration to honor the Philadelphia Eagles and their Super Bowl was scheduled. On June 4, however, President Trump abruptly cancelled the event after learning that several prominent players would not attend in protest of the president's recent criticism of players who knelt during the national anthem.

Trump attributed the decision to cancel the White House ceremony to the team's lack of patriotism. Long and several other Eagles players responded to Trump's accusation, which was repeated numerous times by Fox News and other conservative media outlets, by noting that not one Philadelphia Eagles player had taken a knee in protest during the national anthem before any game during the 2017–2018 season.

Long also criticized NFL Commissioner Roger Goodell for not standing up for the players. "I know my teammates are great men," he said in an interview with reporters. "There's men of faith in this locker room, there's men who serve in their communities, men who have a lot to give back to people with a lot less, and they don't have to do that at all. What the commissioner wants to do, that's not my business" (Rosenblatt 2018).

Further Reading

Chris Long Foundation. 2018. https://chrislongfoundation.org/about/

Hayes, Marcus. 2017. "Eagles' Chris Long Defends Hometown Charlottesville, Blasts Trump." *The Philadelphia Inquirer,* August 13, 2017. http://www.philly.com/philly/columnists/marcus_hayes/philadelphia-eagles-chris-long-hometown-charlottesville-donald-trump-white-supremacy-protest-20170814.html

Kulp, Andrew. 2017. "Chris Long to Malcolm Jenkins: 'I'm Here for You'." *NBC Sports,* August 18, 2017. https://www.nbcsports.com/philadelphia/philadelphia-eagles/chris-long-malcolm-jenkins-im-here-you

Long, Chris. 2018 (@JOEL9ONE). Twitter, May 23, 2018. https://twitter.com/JOE
    L9ONE/status/999408653445795840
Mather, Victor. 2017. "Chris Long of the Philadelphia Eagles to Donate Entire
    Salary." *New York Times,* October 19, 2017. https://www.nytimes.com
    /2017/10/19/sports/football/chris-long-philadelphia-eagles-donation.html
Rosenblatt, Zack. 2018. "Eagles' Chris Long Takes Shot at NFL's Roger Goodell."
    NJ.com, June 7, 2018. https://www.nj.com/eagles/index.ssf/2018/06/eagles_
    chris_long_roger_goodell.html
Zangaro, Dave. 2017. "Not Sticking to Sports, Charlottesville Native Chris Long
    Feels a Responsibility to Speak Out." *NBC Sports,* August 13, 2017. https://
    www.nbcsports.com/philadelphia/philadelphia-eagles/not-sticking-sports
    -charlottesville-native-chris-long-feels-responsibility-speak

Reid, Eric (1991–)

Former teammate of Colin Kaepernick and second NFL player to kneel in protest during the National Anthem

On December 10, 1991, Eric Reid was born in Baton Rouge, Louisiana. In high school, he was accomplished in football, earning an invitation to play in the 2010 All-American Bowl, a game for the best high-school football players in the country. He also excelled as a player at Louisiana State University, earning All-American honors for his performance on the football field. In the 2013 NFL Draft, the San Francisco 49ers picked Reid 18th overall; Reid experienced several successful seasons despite injuries.

In 2016, Reid became the second NFL player to participate in protests during the playing of the national anthem, which aimed to raise awareness of racial and social inequality and police brutality against people of color. The protests began in August when Colin Kaepernick, Reid's teammate on the San Francisco 49ers, sat on the bench during the first few preseason games before the regular season. Within a few weeks, however, Kaepernick's protests evolved into kneeling on the sidelines during the national anthem. Reid joined him.

In an op-ed for the *New York Times,* Reid traced the origins of his decision to join Kaepernick's protest. He chronicled his growing awareness of the issue of police brutality and killings of unarmed African Americans during encounters with law enforcement. In particular, he was affected by the death of Alton Sterling, a young black man shot by two police officers in Reid's hometown of Baton Rouge, Louisiana, on June 5, 2016. Bystanders filmed the tragic incident, and the video sparked widespread outrage and calls for justice. According to Reid's op-ed, Sterling's death and the controversy surrounding it prompted Reid to examine his own conscience, consult his faith, and join Kaepernick's protest.

"I approached Colin the Saturday before our next game to discuss how I could get involved with the cause but also how we could make a more powerful and positive impact on the social justice movement," he recalled. "We spoke at length about many of the issues that face our community, including systematic oppression of people of color, police brutality, and the criminal justice system. We also discussed how we could use our platform, provided to us by being professional athletes in the N.F.L., to speak for those who are voiceless" (Reid 2017).

Reid took a knee alongside Kaepernick during the national anthem at the September 1 game. Over subsequent weeks, the protest expanded to other teams in the league. As the press began to report on the protests, backlash from fans and sponsors who opposed the reasons for and timing of the demonstrations increased. President Trump voiced his opposition to the player movement at a rally in Alabama on September 22, 2017, calling the players unpatriotic and disrespectful to the flag and the military. Moreover, he urged NFL owners to fire any player participating in the protests.

"It baffles me that our protest is still being misconstrued as disrespectful to the country, flag, and military personnel," Reid wrote. "We chose it because it is exactly the opposite. It has always been my understanding that the brave men and women who fought and died for our country did so to ensure that we could live in a fair and free society, which includes the right to speak out in protest" (Reid 2017).

Reid continued to kneel alongside Kaepernick before each game that season. In early August 2017, however, he announced that he would be ending his involvement. To reporters, he explained that the goal of the protests was to raise awareness on issues of racial inequality and police brutality. In his opinion, that goal had been reached.

Reid's views on the national anthem protests changed after the Unite the Right rally in Charlottesville, Virginia, later in August. The rally brought together alt-right activists, white supremacists, and neo-Nazi elements in opposition to the removal of a statue of Confederate general Robert E. Lee from a local park. On the final day of the rally, a far-right activist purposely drove into a group of counter protesters, killing a young woman and injuring many others.

Before the preseason game against the Minnesota Vikings on August 27, 2017, Reid once again took a knee during the national anthem. He explained that he felt it was necessary after the events in Charlottesville to do more to fight for social justice despite the backlash and false narratives against the player protests.

"At first, I thought that was a small sacrifice to pay to get the word out to raise awareness, and I settled with thinking that raising that awareness was a victory," he stated. "Then fast-forward to Charlottesville, and the country sees what an un-American protest looks like. That's when I had my change of heart, because what Colin, Eli [Harold], and I did was a peaceful protest fueled by faith in God to help make our country a better place. And I feel like I need to regain control of that narrative and not let people say that what we're doing is un-American, because it's not. It's completely American" (NFL.com 2017).

After the season, Reid became a free agent. Despite some interest, no team offered him a contract. Although some pro football experts attributed the situation to a strong, competitive free agent market at his position, others speculated as to the role of his vocal social justice activism in his lack of contract offers. Many pointed to the fact that Reid's former teammate, Colin Kaepernick, had not been offered an NFL contract either, despite being a free agent since the start of the 2017 season. In November, Kaepernick had filed a grievance against the NFL and its owners, alleging they were colluding to keep him out of the league because of his political and social justice activism.

Reid indicated that he would be taking a different approach to protests if he were to be signed by an NFL team. "I'm not saying I'm going to stop being active because I won't," he said to reporters. "I'm just going to consider different ways to be active, different ways to bring awareness to the issues of this country and improve on the issues happening to this country. I don't think it will be in the form of protesting during the anthem" (ESPN 2018).

When Kaepernick was awarded the Ambassador of Conscience Award on April 24, 2018, for his social justice activism, Reid was asked to introduce him. In his speech, Kaepernick acknowledged Reid's friendship and support, but he also expressed sorrow that Reid's activism had led to serious professional consequences. "Eric introducing me for this prestigious award brings me joy," he said. "But I am also pained by the fact that his taking a knee and demonstrating courage to protect the rights of Black and brown people in America has also led to his ostracization from the NFL when he is widely recognized as one of the best competitors in the game and in the prime of his career" (Kaepernick 2018).

In May 2018, Reid filed a grievance against the NFL, alleging that the league and its owners had colluded against him because of the anthem protests. On Twitter, Reid criticized teams who devalued him as a player because of his social justice activities. "The notion that I can be a great signing for your team for cheap, not because of my skill set but because I've protested systematic oppression, is ludicrous" (@E_Reid35 March 15, 2018).

Further Reading

ESPN. 2018. "Eric Reid Says He Doesn't Plan to Protest during Anthem, Will Take 'Different Approach'." ESPN, March 23, 2018. http://www.espn.com/nfl/story/_/id/22873957/eric-reid-says-plan-protest-anthem

Kaepernick, Colin. 2018. "Amnesty International's Ambassador of Conscience Award: Transcript of Speech." Amnesty International, April 21, 2018. https://www.amnesty.nl/content/uploads/2018/04/Colin-Kaepernicks-Speech-Ambassador-of-Conscience-Final.pdf?x66178

National Football League. 2017. "Eric Reid: Goal of Anthem Protests Is to Create Change." NFL.com, August 28, 2017. http://www.nfl.com/news/story/0ap3000000835985/article/eric-reid-goal-of-anthem-protests-is-to-create-change

Reid, Eric. 2017. "Why Colin Kaepernick and I Decided to Take a Knee." *New York Times*, September 23, 2017. https://www.nytimes.com/2017/09/25/opinion/colin-kaepernick-football-protests.html

Reid, Eric (@E_Reid35). 2018. Twitter, March 15, 2018. https://twitter.com/E_Reid35/status/974433363061719040

Trump, Donald J. (1946–)

Forty-fifth U.S. president, who made the NFL protests a national political issue by criticizing protesting players

On June 14, 1946, Donald Trump was born in Queens, New York. His father, Fred Trump, was the founder and owner of a successful real estate development and management company, which later became The Trump Organization. After attending Fordham University and the Wharton School at the University of Pennsylvania, Donald joined his father's real estate business. In 1971, he took over, expanding the family business into Manhattan. The Trump Organization expanded into marketing and branding, licensing the Trump name for golf courses, casinos, skyscrapers, and resorts all over the world.

Trump was also involved in other business and entertainment ventures. In 1983, he bought the New Jersey Generals, a team in the fledgling United States Football League. The league folded in 1985. For several years, he owned the Miss Universe pageants and operated a for-profit company called Trump University. He published several books, appeared on TV and in movies, and was the executive producer and host of a popular reality TV show, *The Apprentice,* which ran for several seasons.

On June 16, 2015, Trump announced the launch of his campaign to seek the Republican nomination for President. In the 2016 election, Trump won the nomination and narrowly beat his Democratic challenger, Hillary Clinton, in the electoral college vote. On January 20, 2017, Trump was inaugurated as the 45th president of the United States.

In 2016, Colin Kaepernick, a quarterback for the San Francisco 49ers, attracted nationwide attention for protesting the systematic oppression of people of color by kneeling during the national anthem. Other players were inspired by his actions and joined the protest, which continued into the 2017 season.

The NFL anthem protests caught the president's attention. On September 22, 2017, he criticized protesters during a rally in Alabama, calling the players unpatriotic and disrespectful. Moreover, he urged NFL owners to fire any player participating in the protests. "Wouldn't you love to see one of these NFL owners, when somebody disrespects our flag, to say 'Get that son of a b**** off that field right now! Out! He's fired. He's fired!'" (Graham 2017).

NFL owners reacted swiftly to Trump's remarks. Many stood arm-in-arm with their players during the anthem before the next game as an expression of team unity. Stephen Ross, the owner of the Miami Dolphins, posted a statement that criticized the president's rhetoric. "Our country needs unifying leadership right now, not more divisiveness," it read. "We need to seek to understand each other and have civil discourse instead of condemnation and sound bites. I know our players who kneeled for the anthem and these are smart young men of character who want to make our world a better place for everyone" (@MiamiDolphins September 23, 2017).

When other critics accused Trump of inflaming racial tensions for political purposes, he denied the charge. "This has nothing to do with race," he argued. "I never said anything about race. This has nothing to do with race or anything else. This has to do with respect for our country and respect for our flag" (Tynes 2017).

Polls conducted in the aftermath of the president's remarks showed considerable support for his views. A September 2017 CBS News poll found that 52 percent of Americans disapproved of the NFL anthem protests, while 38 percent approved. In the same poll, results showed that 48 percent had disapproved of Trump's comments, while 38 percent approved (De Pinto et. al. 2017). However, polls also found the president's controversial comments strongly appealed to his Republican base. Over the following months, Trump continued to expand on his earlier comments at rallies and on social media, always arguing that the player protests were disrespectful to the military, the flag, and the country. A number of NFL officials and team owners thought the enduring controversy over the issue was the main reason behind the flat attendance at games during the 2017–2018 NFL season.

Behind the scenes, Trump also exerted political pressure on a few of the NFL owners to revise the existing anthem protest policy. In a court deposition, Dallas Cowboys owner Jerry Jones, a close friend and supporter of President Trump, revealed that the president told him that the NFL would not win on the issue and urged him to implement a tougher policy.

In May, the NFL owners announced they had approved a new national anthem policy that requires players and team personnel to stand if they are on the field during the anthem. Not adhering to those rules could result in a league fine. However, the policy provided the option for the players to remain in the locker room at that time if they preferred.

President Trump expressed his approval of the new anthem protest policy. "I think that's good," he remarked. "I don't think people should be staying in locker rooms but I still think it's good, you have to stand proudly for the national anthem. Or you shouldn't be playing, you shouldn't be there. Maybe you shouldn't be in the country. You have to stand proudly for the national anthem and the NFL owners did the right thing if that's what they've done" (NFL.com 2018).

A few weeks after the policy change, the Philadelphia Eagles were scheduled to visit the White House and meet with President Trump to celebrate their Super Bowl championship. On the day before the scheduled visit, however, Trump cancelled the event after news leaked that several prominent players would not attend because of his criticism of the players' protests.

The president attributed the abrupt cancellation to the team's lack of patriotism. "[The Philadelphia Eagles] disagree with their president because he insists that they proudly stand for the National Anthem, hand on heart, in honor of the great men and women of our military and the people of our country. The Eagles wanted to send a smaller delegation, but the 1,000 fans planning to attend deserve better" (Trump 2018).

The NFL Players Association responded to the cancellation. "Our union is disappointed in the decision by the White House to disinvite players from the Philadelphia Eagles from being recognized and celebrated by all Americans for their accomplishment," the statement read. "This decision by the White House has led to the cancellation of several player-led community service events for young people in the Washington, DC, area. NFL players love their country, support our troops, give back to our communities and strive to make America a better place" (NFLPA 2018).

Further Reading

De Pinto, Jennifer, Fred Backus, Kabir Khanna, and Anthony Salvanto. 2017. "Democrats, Republicans Divide over NFL Protests, Trump Comments—Poll." CBSNews, September 29, 2017. https://www.cbsnews.com/news/democrats-republicans-divide-over-nfl-players-protests-trump-comments-poll/

Graham, Bryan Armen. 2017. "Donald Trump Blasts NFL Anthem Protesters: 'Get That Son of a B**** off the Field'." *The Guardian*, September 23, 2017. https://www.theguardian.com/sport/2017/sep/22/donald-trump-nfl-national-anthem-protests

The Miami Dolphins (@MiamiDolphins). 2017. "Stephen Ross Statement." Twitter, September 23, 2017. https://twitter.com/MiamiDolphins/status/911702747904446465

National Football League. 2018. "Donald Trump: NFL Did the 'Right Thing' with Anthem Policy." NFL, May 24, 2018. http://www.nfl.com/news/story/0ap3000000934197/article/donald-trump-nfl-did-right-thing-with-anthem-policy

National Football League Players Association. 2018. "NFLPA Statement on Philadelphia Eagles White House Visit." NFLPA, June 5, 2018. https://www.nflpa.com/news/nflpa-statement-on-philadelphia-eagles-white-house-visit

Trump, Donald. 2018. "Statement of the President." June 4, 2018. https://www.whitehouse.gov/briefings-statements/statement-by-the-president-2/

Tynes, Tyler. 2017. "Donald Trump Says His Comments on NFL Player Protest 'Have Nothing to Do about Race'." *SB Nation* (blog), September 24, 2017. https://www.sbnation.com/2017/9/24/16358682/donald-trump-says-nfl-protest-anthem-race

Villanueva, Alejandro (1988–)

Pittsburgh Steelers player who stood visibly at the front of the players' tunnel during the National Anthem while teammates remained out of sight inside the tunnel

Alejandro Villaneuva was born on September 22, 1988, in Meridian, Mississippi. His father, Ignacio Villaneuva, was a Spanish naval officer and North Atlantic Treaty Organization official, assigned to Naval Air Station Meridian at the time of Alejandro's birth. Because of his father's career, the family also lived in Rhode Island, Spain, and Belgium during his childhood. While attending high school in Belgium, Villanueva played American football, catching the attention of football coaches at the United States Military Academy at West Point. In college, he played several positions for the Army Black Knights and was voted team captain his senior year.

Villaneuva was not selected in the 2010 NFL Draft. After an unsuccessful tryout with the Cincinnati Bengals, he returned to military duty. He spent a year in Afghanistan as part of Operation Enduring Freedom, receiving a Bronze Star. In 2013, he volunteered for service in the Rangers and was deployed again to Afghanistan.

After he left the military, Villaneuva attended regional NFL scouting combines in a few cities and was eventually picked up by the Pittsburgh Steelers, where he spent the season on the practice squad. His continual improvement on and off the field and noted work ethic earned him recognition from coaches and teammates and ultimately a starting position during the 2016 season.

Both a military veteran and an NFL player, Villaneuva has a unique perspective on the NFL anthem controversy. Villaneuva agreed with the reasons for protest, but disagreed with the forum chosen by Kaepernick and other players to do it. "I think he's obviously upset and I think we all agree, I think the majority of America would all agree that there's an issue with minorities in our country and the way that certain groups in our population are being treated," he stated. "I just think that shotgun blast and not standing up for America is a little bit unfair on his part because it's not really taking into consideration the minorities that are fighting for the flag, like myself—the thousands of people that are laying their lives to make sure that he can express himself" (Klinger 2016).

At a rally in Alabama on September 22, 2017, President Donald Trump blasted NFL protesters, contending that owners should fire any player who took a knee during the anthem for being disrespectful to the flag, the military, and the nation.

In reaction to the president's statement, the Pittsburgh Steelers voted as a team to stay in the tunnel during the playing of the national anthem before the next scheduled game with the Chicago Bears at Soldier Field in Chicago. Although they had always stood as a team during the anthem before, the political controversy led to the change in plans. The decision was made because the team wanted to avoid the controversy, not out of protest. "We decided we were going to sit it out, we weren't going to play politics," Pittsburgh Steelers head coach Mike Tomlin stated. "They decided to stay in the tunnel and not play politics of any kind" (Dulac 2017).

Villanueva recalls consulting with Steelers team captains Ben Roethlisberger and Cam Heyward at the last minute as to whether he could stand at the front of the tunnel while the national anthem played, so that he could see the flag. Given the go ahead, Villanueva found himself alone at the front the tunnel during the anthem, where he could be seen by fans and TV cameras. He tried to signal his teammates to join him at the front of the tunnel for the anthem, but he was blocked by other personnel. By that time, he claimed, it would have looked bad to walk to the back of the tunnel to rejoin his teammates.

The striking image of Villanueva standing alone during the national anthem with his hand over his heart catapulted him into the national spotlight. Many fans incorrectly assumed that he had taken a stand against the protests. For fans and commentators who did not approve of the protesters' actions, Villanueva was viewed as a hero. Sales of his Pittsburgh Steelers jersey skyrocketed, ending the season ranked the 30th most popular jersey in the NFL. Villanueva donated the money to various charities in Pittsburgh and three other cities.

A few days after the game, Villanueva explained how the situation occurred. "When everybody sees the image of me by myself, everybody thinks the team, the Steelers, are not behind me, and that's absolutely wrong," he said to reporters (Fowler 2017).

"I see that picture of me standing by myself and I'm embarrassed to a degree, because unintentionally I left my teammates behind. It wasn't me stepping forward. I never planned to boycott. . . . At the end of the day, whether I want it or not, the reason I went out there by myself is the reason it's causing all this distress" (Fowler, 2017).

In the incident's aftermath, Villanueva received support from coaches and teammates. Tomlin told reporters Villanueva had "nothing to apologize for" (Dulac 2017). Roethlisberger posted a reflection on Facebook, contending that he wished the team had handled the controversy differently and that the national anthem was not the right time for protest (Rapaport 2017).

The controversy did provide Villanueva a chance to learn more about the divisive issue. "I can't tell you I know what my teammates have gone through, so I'm not going to pretend like I have the righteous sort of voice to tell you that you should stand up for the national anthem," he stated. "It's protected by our constitution and our country. It's the freedom of speech. People felt, based on the comments the president made, they had to go out and protect and support Colin Kaepernick, and that's completely in their right. But it is not something we were trying to do with the Steelers. We were trying to be unified" (Fowler 2017).

Further Reading

Dulac, Gerry. 2017. "Mike Tomlin: Alejandro Villanueva Has 'Nothing to Apologize for'." *Pittsburgh Post-Gazette,* September 26, 2017. http://www.post-gazette.com/sports/steelers/2017/09/26/mike-tomlin-steelers-anthem-protest-alejandro-villanueva-nfl-donald-trumo/stories/201709260118

Fowler, Jeremy. 2017. "Alejandro Villaueuva Sorry for Making Steelers Look Bad by Standing Alone." ESPN, September 26, 2017. http://www.espn.com/nfl/story/_/id/20819284/alejandro-villanueva-pittsburgh-steelers-standing-alone-intentional

Klinger, Jacob. 2016. "Pittsburgh Steeler, Army Vet Alejandro Villaneuva Agrees with Kaepernick, Not His Protest." *PennLive*, August 29, 2016. https://www.pennlive.com/steelers/index.ssf/2016/08/steelers_villanueva_kaepernick.html

Rapaport, Daniel. 2017. "Ben Roethlisberger on Steelers Sitting out Anthem: 'I Wish We Approached It Differently'." *Sports Illustrated*, September 25, 2017. https://www.si.com/nfl/2017/09/25/ben-roethlisberger-pittsburgh-steelers-national-anthem-protest

Further Resources

Sports and Protest Movements

Bennett, Michael. 2018. *Things That Make White People Uncomfortable.* Chicago: Haymarket Books.

Bryant, Howard. 2018. *The Heritage: Black Athletes, a Divided America and the Politics of Patriotism.* Boston: Beacon Press.

Edwards, Harry. 2018. *The Revolt of the Black Athlete.* 50th Anniversary Ed. Champaign, IL: University of Illinois Press.

Farmer, Ashley. 2016. "Black Women Athletes, Protest, and Politics: An Interview with Amira Rose Davis." *Black Perspectives,* October 14, 2016. https://www.aaihs.org/black-women-athletes-protest-and-politics-an-interview-with-amira-rose-davis/

French, David. 2017. "Politicize Sports, Pay the Price." *National Review,* July 29, 2017. https://www.nationalreview.com/2017/07/nfl-colin-kaepernick-national-anthem-survey-fans-tuned-out/

Hall, Peter. 2010. *American Patriotism, American Protest.* Philadelphia: University of Pennsylvania Press.

Johnk, Zach. 2017. "National Anthem Protests by Black Athletes Have a Long History." *New York Times,* September 25, 2017. https://www.nytimes.com/2017/09/25/sports/national-anthem-protests-black-athletes.html

Kafka, Peter. 2017. "#TakeAKnee Is New, Sports Have Always Been Political, Says the WSJ's Jason Gay." *Recode with Peter Kafka,* Podcast audio, October 5, 2017. https://www.recode.net/2017/10/5/16424486/jason-gay-wall-street-journal-politics-sports-kaepernick-nfl-anthem-protests-peter-kafka-podcast

Kupfer, Theodore. 2017. "Can't We All Just Stick to Sports?" *National Review,* August 23, 2017. https://www.nationalreview.com/2017/08/espn-politicizing-sports-fans-should-ignore-it/

Large, David Clay. 2012. *Munich 1972: Tragedy, Terror, and Triumph at the Olympic Games.* Lanham, MD: Rowman & Littlefield.

Lipsyte, Robert. 2018. "Donald Trump's War on Black Athletes." *The Nation,* July 12, 2018. https://www.thenation.com/article/donald-trumps-war-sports/

Newkirk, Vann R., II. 2017. "Football Has Always Been a Battleground in the Culture War." *The Atlantic,* September 29, 2017. https://www.theatlantic.com/politics/archive/2017/09/football-is-the-culture-war/541464/

Thomas, Etan. 2018. *We Matter: Athletes and Activism.* Brooklyn, NY: Edge of Sports/Akashic Publishing.

Vasilogambros, Matt. 2016. "When Athletes Take Political Stands." *The Atlantic,* July 20, 2016. https://www.theatlantic.com/news/archive/2016/07/when-athletes-take-political-stands/490967/

Waldron, Travis. 2017. "The NFL Has Always Been Political." *Huffington Post,* September 25, 2017. https://www.huffingtonpost.com/entry/nfl-football-political_us_59c91815e4b06ddf45f9b002

Werner, Barry. 2016. "Colin Kaepernick's Protest at the Intersection of Patriotism and Athletics Is Far from New." *FoxSports.com,* October 20, 2016. https://www.foxsports.com/nfl/story/colin-kaepernicks-protest-at-the-intersection-of-patriotism-and-athletics-is-far-from-new-083116

NFL Protests and Social Justice Issues

Abdurraqib, Hanif. 2018. "How I Said Goodbye to the NFL." *Pacific Standard,* June 1, 2018. https://psmag.com/social-justice/how-i-said-goodbye-to-the-nfl

"The Anthem/Balls and Strikes/Magic Man." 2016. *Real Sports with Bryant Gumbel,* season 22, episode 9, produced by Tim Walker (segment), starring Bryant Gumbel, aired on September 27, 2016, on HBO.

Barbaro, Michael. 2017. "Protest on the NFL Sidelines." *New York Times,* Podcast audio, September 25, 2017. https://www.nytimes.com/2017/09/25/podcasts/the-daily/donald-trump-nfl-national-anthem.html

Bouie, Jamelle. 2018. "Taking a Stand." *Slate.com,* May 24, 2018. https://slate.com/news-and-politics/2018/05/nfl-anthem-policy-league-sides-with-donald-trumps-campaign-against-black-political-power.html

Branch, John. 2017. "The Awakening of Colin Kaepernick." *New York Times Magazine,* September 7, 2017. https://www.nytimes.com/2017/09/07/sports/colin-kaepernick-nfl-protests.html

Bryant, Howard. 2018. "A Protest Divided." *ESPN Podcenter,* Podcast audio, March 21, 2018. http://www.espn.com/espnradio/play?id=22855350

Chapman, Mark. 2017. "On Bended Knee: NFL Protest Special." *BBC Sports: 5 Live Sports Specials,* Podcast audio, October 11, 2018. https://www.bbc.co.uk/programmes/p05jph9x

Coaston, Jane. 2018. "2 Years of NFL Protests, Explained." *Vox,* August 15, 2018. https://www.vox.com/2018/8/15/17619122/kaepernick-trump-nfl-protests-2018

Coates, Ta-Nehisi. 2017. "Civil-Rights Protests Have Never Been Popular." *The Atlantic,* October 3, 2017. https://www.theatlantic.com/politics/archive/2017/10/colin-kaepernick/541845/

Crouch, Ian. 2018. "The Indignity of the N.F.L.'s New National-Anthem Policy." *The New Yorker,* May 24, 2018. https://www.newyorker.com/news/sporting-scene/the-indignity-of-the-nfls-new-national-anthem-policy

Green, Marcus Harrison. 2018. "Social Justice vs. the NFL." *Seattle Weekly,* May 30, 2018. http://www.seattleweekly.com/opinion/social-justice-vs-the-nfl/

Hayes, Chris. 2017. *A Colony in a Nation.* New York: W.W. Norton & Co.

Leah, Rachel. 2017. "So What Would It Look Like If the NFL Forced Players to Stand?" *Salon,* October 15, 2017. https://www.salon.com/2017/10/15/so-what-it-look-like-if-the-nfl-forced-players-to-stand/

Lebron, Christopher J. 2017. *The Making of Black Lives Matter: A Brief History of an Idea.* New York: Oxford University Press.

Leibovich, Mark. 2018. *Big Game: The NFL in Dangerous Times.* New York: Penguin Press.

Lipsyte, Robert. 2017. "Is Donald Trump Saving the NFL?" *The Nation,* October 19, 2017. https://www.thenation.com/article/is-donald-trump-saving-the-nfl/

Newkirk, Vann R., II. 2017. "No Country for Colin Kaepernick." *The Atlantic,* August 11, 2017. https://www.theatlantic.com/entertainment/archive/2017/08/no-country-for-colin-kaepernick/536340/

Pegue, Jeff. 2017. *Black and Blue: Inside the Divide between the Police and Black America.* Amherst, NY: Prometheus Books.

Smith, Jamil. 2018. "The NFL Panders to Trump." *Rolling Stone,* May 24, 2018. https://www.rollingstone.com/politics/politics-features/the-nfl-panders-to-trump-627884/

Wilmore, Larry. 2017. "Michael Bennett on NFL Protests and Fans Not Seeing Football Players as Human: Episode 16." *Black on the Air,* Podcast audio, October 8, 2017. https://www.theringer.com/nfl/2017/10/8/16444248/michael-bennett-nfl-protests

Zirin, Dave. 2018. "Andrew Brandt on Kaepernick and the Business of the NFL." *Edge of Sports with Dave Zirin.* Podcast audio, February 20, 2018. http://www.edgeofsportspodcast.com/article/andrew-brandt-on-colin-kaepernick-and-the-business-of-the-nfl/

Patriotism and Protest

Beauchamp, Zack. 2017. "It's Actually Very Strange for Sports Games to Begin with the National Anthem." *Vox,* September 25, 2017. https://www.vox.com/2016/9/3/12774172/colin-kaepernick-national-anthem-why

Brady, Erik. 2017. "How National Anthem Became Essential Part of Sports." *USA Today,* September 26, 2017. https://www.usatoday.com/story/sports/nfl/2017/09/26/how-national-anthem-become-essential-part-sports/706243001/

Cavanaugh, Ray. 2016. "The Star-Spangled Banner: An American Anthem with a Very British Beginning." *The Guardian,* July 4, 2016.

https://www.theguardian.com/music/2016/jul/04/star-spangled-banner
-national-anthem-british-originshttps://www.theguardian.com/music/
2016/jul/04/star-spangled-banner-national-anthem-british-origins

Cowen, Tyler. 2017. "Dial Down the National Anthem at Sporting Events." *Bloomberg,* September 25, 2017. https://www.bloomberg.com/view/articles/
2017-09-25/dial-down-the-national-anthem-at-sporting-events

Cyphers, Luke, and Ethan Trex. 2011. "The Song Remains the Same." *ESPN The Magazine,* September 19, 2011. http://www.espn.com/espn/story/_/id/
6957582/the-history-national-anthem-sports-espn-magazine

Ferris, Marc. 2014. *Star-Spangled Banner: The Unlikely Story of America's National Anthem.* Baltimore: Johns Hopkins University Press.

Flake, Jeff, and John McCain. 2015. *Tackling Paid Patriotism: A Joint Oversight Report,* 2015. https://www.mccain.senate.gov/public/_cache/files/
12de6dcb-d8d8-4a58-8795-562297f948c1/tackling-paid-patriotism
-oversight-report.pdf

Kumagai, Jillian. 2015. "What Makes a Great National Anthem?" *The Atlantic,* September 15, 2015. https://www.theatlantic.com/international/archive/2015/
09/national-anthems-alex-marshall/405304/

Lowry, Rich. 2017. "No Way to Treat Old Glory." *National Review,* September 26, 2017. https://www.nationalreview.com/2017/09/nfl-national-anthem
-protests-american-flag-deserves-more-respect/

McLaughlin, Dan. 2017. "Flag Protests and the Power of Symbols." *National Review,* October 11, 2017. https://www.nationalreview.com/2017/10/
national-anthem-confederate-flag-besieged-symbols-unserious-time/

Ng, David. 2016. "How 'The Star-Spangled Banner,' Racist or Not, Became Our National Anthem." *Los Angeles Times,* September 6, 2016. http://
www.latimes.com/entertainment/arts/la-et-cm-star-spangled-banner-racism
-20160823-snap-story.html

Olson, Walter. 2017. "Is 'The Star-Spangled Banner' Racist?" *National Review,* September 15, 2017. https://www.nationalreview.com/2017/09/star-spangled
-banner-racist-anthem/

Resnick, Brian. 2014. "The National Anthem Was Set to the Tune of a British Drinking Song." *The Atlantic,* May 14, 2014. https://www.theatlantic.com/
politics/archive/2014/05/the-national-anthem-was-set-to-the-tune-of-a
-british-drinking-song/453693/

Staples, Brent. 2018. "African-Americans and the Strains of the National Anthem." *New York Times,* June 9, 2018. https://www.nytimes.com/2018/06/09/opin
ion/african-americans-national-anthem-protests.html

Watkins, D. 2017. "How Much Do Offended People Really Love the National Anthem?" *Salon,* December 9, 2017. https://www.salon.com/2017/12/09/
how-much-do-offended-white-people-really-love-the-national-anthem/

What So Proudly We Hail. Directed by Duane Sanders Jr. 2016. Morgan State University, Vimeo. https://vimeo.com/166881889

Index

Abdul-Jabbar, Kareem, 2, 87
Abdul-Rauf, Mahmoud, 2, 69;
    aftermath of protest, 28–29; protest,
    origin of, 27–28
African American athletes: baseball
    players, 70–71; during 1968 and
    1972 Summer Olympics, 2; NFL's
    new policy and, 7–8; social injustice
    and racial issues and, 2–3; "The
    Star-Spangled Banner," 11; Trump's
    attitude toward, 6–7. *See also
    specific players*
African Americans: black power
    movement, 21; civil rights
    movement, 21; Garner's death and,
    5; killings by police officers, 4–5, 85;
    in Mizzou Football Team, 39–40;
    racism in criminal sentencing and,
    4–5; 2012 Martin case and, 4–5;
    violence against, 37
Ali, Muhammad, 2, 21
American Civil Liberties Union (ACLU),
    75
*Anthem—The Story behind "The
    Star-Spangled Banner,"* 16
Anti-gay discrimination, 37
Armour, Nancy, 74
Army Times, 42, 96, 111
Attiah, Karen, 82
Austin, Tavon, 3, 34

Bademosi, Johnson, 102
Bailey, Stedman, 3, 34
Baltimore Harbor, 16
Baltimore Orioles, 70
Barr, Roseanne, 19
Bass, Mistie, 70
Baton Rouge, Louisiana, 41
Battle of Bladensburg, 77
Bausby, De'Vante, 103
Beachum, Kelvin, 105
Bennett, Michael, 103
Berrett, Jesse, 89
Bettman, Gary, 71
Bisciotti, Steve, 47
Black power movement, 21
Boldin, Anquan, 102
Bone, Kelsey, 70
Borders, Lisa, 69
Bowerman, Bill, 26
Boyer, Nate, 42, 80, 95–97, 111;
    awards, 95; and Colin Kaepernick,
    96–97; education, 95; and Eric
    Reid, 96–97; #TakeAKnee protests
    by, 96–97
Britt, Kenny, 3, 34
Brooks, Ron, 102
Brown, J. T., 71
Brown, Michael, 3, 5, 33, 37, 85
Brundage, Avery, 21, 25
Burbank, Stephen, 113

Burns, Artie, 52
Butler, Jonathan, 37, 38–39

Carlos, John, 2, 20
Caucasian Americans, 28
CBS/YouGov poll, 81
Chait, Jonathan, 66
Chan, Jennifer Lee, 1, 41
Chicago Tribune, 12, 13
Civil rights movement, 21
Civil War, 12
Clague, Mark, 78–79
Cleveland Browns, 103
Cleveland Cavaliers, 68
"The Code for the National Anthem
    of the United States," 17
Cole, David, 75
Collett, Wayne, 2, 23–26
Cook, Jared, 3, 34
Corporate sponsors: NFL protests and,
    59–60; Nike's controversial ad
    campaign, 62–63; Papa John's Pizza
    case and, 61–62
Corporate sponsorship: financial value
    of, 60; Papa John's Pizza case, 60–61;
    Nike's controversial ad campaign,
    62–63
Cruz, Ted, 65
Curry, Steph, 69

Daily Stormer, 61
Dallas Cowboys, 48, 107–9
Dallas News, 109
Davis, Demario, 105
Denver Nuggets, 2, 27
Department of Defense (DoD), 3,
    31–32
Dominis, John, 22

Elliot, Benjamin, 36

Feliciano, Jose, 16
Fergie, 16
Ferguson incident, 37–38

Fisher, Jeff, 35–36
Fitzgerald, Sean, 36
Flake, Jeff, 3
Foles, Nick, 56
Fort McHenry, 16, 77, 79
Fouse, David, 74
French, David, 75

Gaines/Oldham Black Cultural Center,
    36
Garber, Megan, 85
Garner, Eric, 5, 68, 85
Geragos, Mark, 112
Givens, Chris, 3, 34
Goodell, Roger, 50, 55, 90, 98–100;
    education, 98; new NFL Personal
    Conduct Policy, 98–99; NFL protest
    and, 99–100
Great Lakes Naval Training Center
    band, 13
Green Bay Packers, 41
The Guardian, 4, 85

"Hands Up, Don't Shoot" protest, 3,
    34–35
Head, Payton, 37
Hendrix, Jimmy, 16
Heyward, Cam, 128
Higgins, Clay, 64
Hildebrand, Mark, 16
Hoover, Herbert, 16
House Judiciary Committee, 15
Houston, Whitney, 16
H.R. 14, 15, 16
HuffPost/YouGov poll, 81
Hurricane Maria, 64

#IAMWITHKAP t-shirts, 48
Indiana Fever team, 70
Islam, 2, 27

Jackson, Chris. *See* Abdul-Rauf,
    Mahmoud
Jacksonville Jaguars, 51

James, LeBron, 3, 68, 69
Jenkins, Malcolm, 56, 101–4
Jones, Jerry, 107–9
Johnson, Christopher, 53, 64,
    104–6

Kaepernick, Colin, 110–14; ad
    campaign, 62; awards, 112; early life,
    110; foundation, 112; NBA players
    support for, 69; Nike's ad and,
    113–14; protest, 1, 5–6, 41–42;
    refusal to stand for national anthem,
    41–43; #TakeAKnee demonstrations
    and, 42–43, 48, 80; Trump on,
    44–45
Kerr, Steve, 91
Key, Francis Scott, 12, 16, 77
Khan, Shad, 51
King, Martin Luther, 66
King, Peter, 64
King, Shaun, 78
Koetter, Dirk, 52
Koran, 27
Kraft, Robert, 115–17

Layden, Elmer, 3, 18, 19
Legend, John, 76
Legion of Black Collegians, 38
Linthicum, John, 12, 15
Lockhart, P. R., 91
Loftin, R. Bowen, 38
Long, Chris, 55, 117–20
Los Angeles Sparks, 70
Louisville, Kentucky, 44
Lurie, Jeff, 55

Major League Baseball (MLB), 31,
    70–71
Major League Soccer (MLS),
    71–72
Manning, Peyton, 60
Martin, Trayvon, 4–5
Matthews, Vince, 2, 23–26
Maxwell, Bruce, 71

McCain, John, 3, 64
McCarthy, Brian, 32, 35
McCown, Josh, 105
McDonald, Laquan, 85
McNair, Bob, 49
McNear, Claire, 92
Means, Steve, 102
Miami Dolphins, 53
Middleton, Michael, 36
Monday Night Football, 19, 29

National anthem: CBS policy on, 8;
    corporate sponsors and, 59–60;
    debate, 15–16; Francis Scott Key's
    poem as, 77; Kaepernick kneeling
    during, 6, 43; Kaepernick's refusal
    to stand for, 41–43; legislation,
    introduction of, 15; Malcolm Jenkins
    and, 101–104; Megan Rapinoe
    kneeling during, 71–72; MLB players
    kneeling during, 70–71; MLS
    policies toward, 71–72; NBA's
    policy on, 27; NFL and, 17–18, 19;
    NFL mandates players on field for,
    29–30; NFL players kneeling during,
    7, 86–87; NFL's policy shift on,
    75–76; Nike's ad camp and, 62–63;
    Papa John's Pizza case, 60–61;
    policy, confusion over, 31; race and
    history of, 77; Roger Goodell new
    policy, 98–99; as symbol of
    patriotism, 76; technology and,
    18–19; USSF policies toward, 71–72
National Basketball Association (NBA),
    2, 27, 31, 68–69, 91
National Football League (NFL): and
    Abdul-Rauf's protest, 27–28; brand
    strategy, 88–89; confusion over
    national anthem policy, 31; game
    operations manual, 30; image and
    popularity, 88; and Kaepernick's
    protest, 1, 5–6, 41–43; mandates
    players on field for national anthem,
    29–30; mandatory injunction of

national anthem before games by, 17–18; national anthem policy and, 18, 19, 27; and national politics, 64–65; new anthem policy (2018), 50–53, 82; paid patriotism controversies, 3, 31–32; policy change regarding national anthem, 49–50, 75–76; political partisanship, role of, 6–7; protest, origin of, 4–5, 80, 84–85; public opinion polls on protest, 66–67, 81–82; relationship with U.S. military, 3; Republican opposition to protest, 6–7; reviewing national anthem policy, 7–8; Rulebook, 30, 32; St. Louis Rams protest of 2014, 33, 34–35; Trump's criticisms on protests, 43–45, 46–48, 62–63, 80–81, 82–83; 2009 national anthem policy, 32. *See also* NFL new anthem policy; NFL players

National Football League Players Association (NFLPA), 8, 49, 52, 56

National Hockey League (NHL), 31, 70–71

New England Patriots, 54

Newsday, 106

New York Jets, 51, 103, 105

New York Times, 13

NFL new anthem policy, 75–76; concerns about, 52; overview of, 50–51; reconsidering, 53; support for, 51–52

NFL players: debates on protest, 73; image and popularity, 87–88, 89, 91; NBA players support for, 68–69; patriotic protest, 72–73; patriotism and, 7–8; protesting institutional racism, 32; racial inequality and, 80; right of, 75; and #TakeAKnee demonstrations, 6–7; Trump on protesting, 43–45; Trump's criticism of, 64–65, 74, 80–81, 82–83; Trump's culture war and, 67;

unpatriotic protest, 74; WNBA players and, 69–70

Nike, 62–63, 113

NinersNation.com, 1, 41

Norman, Peter, 22

Oakland Raiders, 34, 117

Olympics of 1968, 2; black power salute at, 20–23; boycotting, 21; context for protest, 20–21; John Carlos, 20–23, and Tommie Smith, 20–23

Olympics of 1972, 2; controversies during, 24–25; medal ceremony, 24; political protest at, 23–26; USOC, 25–26; and Vince Matthews, 23–26; and Wayne Collett, 23–26

"One Mizzou" campaign, 37

O'Rourke, Beto, 8, 64–65

Paid patriotism controversies, 31–32, 89–90

Pantaleo, Daniel, 5

Papa John's Pizza case, 60–61

Patriotism: debates on, 73; NFL new policy and, 75–76; and NFL players, 7–8; paid, 3, 31–32, 89–90; political debate over, 65–66; symbols of, 17, 76

Paul, Chris, 3, 69

Pence, Karen, 48–49

Pence, Mike, 48–49

Philadelphia Eagles, 54, 55–57, 120, 126

Phoenix Mercury players, 70

The Players Coalition, 102

Pittsburgh Steelers, 48, 52

Police brutality, 33, 37, 70, 84, 85–86

Public opinion poll, 66–67, 81–82

Racial discrimination, 37–38, 80, 84, 85–86

Ragland, James, 109

Rapinoe, Megan, 71–72
Real Sports, 96
Red Sox, 12–13
Reid, Eric, 6, 42, 85, 121–23; Alton
    Sterling's death and, 121; Colin
    Kaepernick and, 122; NFL
    and, 123
Rhodesia, 21
Rice, Tamir, 86
Ripley, Robert, 15
Ripley's Believe It or Not!, 15
Roethlisberger, Ben, 128
Roorda, Jeff, 35
Ross, Richard, 102
Russell, Bill, 2
Ruth, Babe, 12

Sacramento Kings, 28
San Jose University, 21
Scher, Bill, 67
Schnatter, John, 61
Schwab, Frank, 62
Seattle Seahawks, 48
Shooting in Ferguson, 37
Skinner, Sam, 25
Smith, Tommie, 2, 20
Social media: debates in, 37–38;
    Ferguson incident and, 37–38;
    memes on, 32; NFL protests on,
    6; NFL's new policy and, 8; and
    Trayvon Martin case, 5; Trump's
    culture war and, 67; WNBA teams
    about police brutality on, 70
Sousa, John Philip, 16
Sport: banning national anthem
    in, 78; MLS and USSF policies
    toward national anthem, 71–72;
    rise of black activism and protest
    in, 1–3
Stallworth, Donte, 102
"The Star-Spangled Banner," 11–57;
    to honor American troops, 12–13;
    J. T. Brown and, 71; as national
    anthem, 15; race and history of, 76;

rise of, 11–12; role of technology,
    18–19; sporting event during
    1918, 11; support for, 78–79;
    War of 1812 and, 16; World Series
    (1918), 12–13. *See also* National
    anthem
Starr, Terrell Jermaine, 78
Sterling, Alton, 5, 41, 84
Stern, David, 28, 69
St. Louis, Missouri: Ferguson incident,
    33–34; "Hands Up, Don't Shoot"
    Protest, 34–35; NFL reaction to
    player protest, 35–36; St. Louis Rams
    protest of 2014, 33, 34–35
St. Louis Police Officers Association
    (SLPOA), 35
Suggs, Terrell, 47
Super Bowl Championship, 54–57,
    60

#TakeAKnee protests, 6, 7, 8,
    70, 80
Tampa Bay Buccaneers, 52
Tampa Bay Lightning, 71
Taylor, Zachary, 36
Technology, and national anthem,
    18–19
Thomas, Fred, 13
Tomlin, Mike, 128
Tourette's syndrome, 27
Transgender discrimination, 37
Trump, Donald J., 6, 32, 124–26;
    attacks on Kaepernick and
    NFL, 44, 67; criticisms of NFL
    protests, 43–45, 74, 80–81, 82–83,
    125; culture war, 67; handling of
    racial issues, 81–82; Nike's ad
    campaign and, 62–63; NFL's
    response to, 46–48; public opinion
    polls on protests and, 66–67, 81–82,
    125; supported new anthem protest
    policy, 51, 126; use of patriotism,
    65–66
Turkish Basketball League, 28

University of Missouri, 5; Butler's hunger strike, 38–39; Ferguson shooting, 37; football team, 39–40; homecoming parade, 38–39; "One Mizzou" campaign, 37; protest of 2015, 36–40; "Racism Lives Here" rallies, 38
University of Texas, 95
University of Virginia, 118
USA Today, 102
U.S. Bank Stadium, 54
U.S. Navy Band, 16
U.S. Olympic Committee (USOC), 22, 25
U.S. Soccer Federation, 71–72
U.S. Supreme Court, 2

Vancouver Grizzlies, 28
Varga, Andrew, 60

Vietnam War, 2, 20, 21, 88–89
Villaneuva, Alejandro, 48, 127–29

Wade, Dwyane, 3, 69
War of 1812, 16
White House, and Super Bowl Championship celebration, 54–57
Williams, John, 16
Willingham, A. J., 80
Wilson, Darren, 3, 5, 33, 37, 85
Wilson, Woodrow, 12
Wolfe, Tim, 5, 38–39
Women's National Basketball Association (WNBA), 69–70
World Series (1918), 12–13
World War I, 12, 16
World War II, 17, 18, 89

Zimmerman, George, 4–5

About the Author

Margaret Haerens is a writer and researcher who has written extensively on American politics, policy, and history.